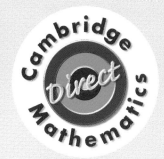

Measures, Shape, Space and Handling Data

CAMBRIDGE
UNIVERSITY PRESS

PUBLISHED BY THE PRESS SYNDICATE OF THE UNIVERSITY OF CAMBRIDGE
The Pitt Building, Trumpington Street, Cambridge, United Kingdom

CAMBRIDGE UNIVERSITY PRESS
The Edinburgh Building, Cambridge CB2 2RU, UK
40 West 20th Street, New York, NY 10011-4211, USA
10 Stamford Road, Oakleigh, VIC 3166, Australia
Ruiz de Alarcón 13, 28014 Madrid, Spain
Dock House, The Waterfront, Cape Town 8001, South Africa

http://www.cambridge.org

First published 2001

Printed in the United Kingdom at the University Press, Cambridge

Typefaces Frutiger, Helvetica, Minion, Swift *System* QuarkXPress®4.03

A catalogue record for this book is available from the British Library

ISBN 0 521 78485 9 paperback

Text illustration Gary Rees

General editors for Cambridge Mathematics Direct
Sandy Cowling, Jane Crowden, Andrew King, Jeanette Mumford

Writing team for *Measures, Shape, Space and Handling Data 5*
Anne Barber, Pete Crawford, Roger Gee, Paul Harrison, Sue Hood, Bob La Roche, Jeanette Mumford, Mary Nathan,
Marian Reynolds, Madeline Swarbrick, Allison Toogood, Elizabeth Toohig, Jane Webster, Joanne Woodward

The writers and publishers would like to thank the many schools and
individuals who trialled lessons for Cambridge Mathematics Direct.

Abbreviations and symbols

IP Interactive picture

CM Copymaster

A is practice work

B develops ideas

C is extension work

★ if needed, helps with work in A

A red margin indicates that activities are teacher-led.

A green margin indicates that activities are independent.

Contents

M 1.1 Measuring and drawing lines in millimetres

> **Key idea** | 75 mm, 7 cm 5 mm and 7.5 cm are equivalent lengths.

A1 In each triangle the parallel lines are drawn from the midpoints of the sides.
Measure the parallel lines to the nearest millimetre.
Write each measurement in 3 different ways.

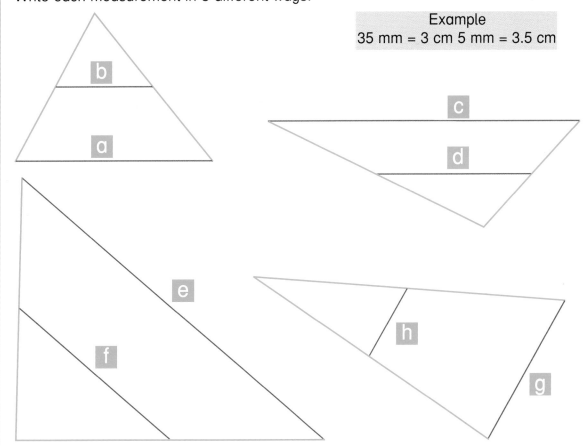

Example
35 mm = 3 cm 5 mm = 3.5 cm

A2 Write what you notice about the lengths of each pair of parallel lines.

B1 Draw lines which are 3.5 cm longer than the lines a, c, e and g in A1.
Write each measurement in 3 different ways.

B2 Draw 4 more zigzag lines
of total length 100 mm.

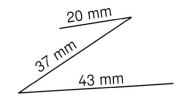

20 mm + 37 mm + 43 mm = 100 mm

C1 Measure the length of these lines to the nearest millimetre.

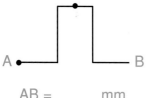

AB = _____ mm

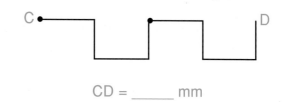

CD = _____ mm

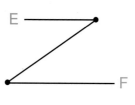

EF = _____ mm

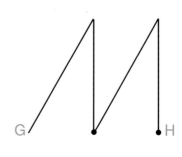

GH = _____ mm

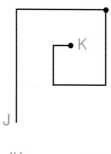

JK = _____ mm

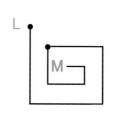

LM = _____ mm

C2 Estimate then measure the **shortest** distance between the two dots on each line. Copy and complete the table.

Line	Estimated distance between dots	Distance between dots to nearest mm
AB		
CD		
Ef		
GH		
JK		
LM		

Key idea | 75 mm, 7 cm 5 mm and 7.5 cm are equivalent lengths.

M1.2 Converting metres to smaller units

Key idea | You can write the same length in several ways.

★1

Copy and complete these diagrams.

| a | is the same length as | | b | is the same length as |

a is the same length as

3 m ←→ 300 cm

2m ←→ ☐ cm

0.3 m ←→ ☐ cm

0.2 m ←→ ☐ cm

b is the same length as

3 m ←→ 3000 mm

2 m ←→ ☐ mm

0.3 m ←→ ☐ mm

0.2 m ←→ ☐ mm

A1

Write these lengths in centimetres.
For example, 3.5 m = 350 cm.

a 1.3 m   b 2.8 m   c 6.6 m

d 24 m   e 57 m   f 90 m

B1

French bread is sold in different lengths.

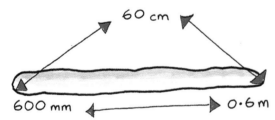

60 cm

600 mm ←→ 0·6 m

For each type of bread, draw a triangle and write the relationship in 3 ways.

 a 500 mm   b 40 cm    c 0·8 m

 d 700 mm    e 65 cm   f 0·9 m

B2 Write these widths in millimetres.
For example, $\frac{1}{10}$ m = 100 mm.

a $\frac{1}{4}$ m

b $\frac{1}{2}$ m

c $\frac{3}{10}$ m

d $\frac{9}{10}$ m

e 0.4 m

f 0.8 m

B3 Panes of glass are measured in millimetres.
Write the dimensions of these window panes in centimetres.

Example
500 mm = 50 cm

a
400 mm
400 mm

b
700 mm
800 mm

c
550 mm
650 mm

B4 The glazier is putting new panes of glass in the front door. Each pane of glass is 300 mm long and 250 mm wide.

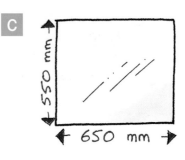

300 mm
250 mm

Work out in metres

a the total height of glass in the door,

b the total width of glass in the door.

C1

You need centimetre squared paper.

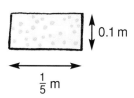

0.1 m

$\frac{1}{5}$ m

All these paving stones are the same size.
You can make these
patterns with 3 stones.

 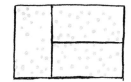 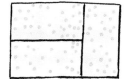

a Here are two 4-stone patterns.
Find 3 more arrangements.
They must be rectangular.

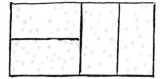 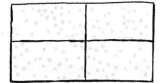

b How many different 5-stone patterns can you find?

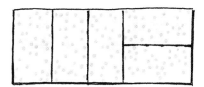

Key idea You can write the same length in several ways.

M 1.3 Metric and imperial units

> **Key idea** | A mile is a bit more than 1.5 km. A mile is about 1600 m.

★1 Copy and complete:

Imperial	Metric
1 mile	1.6 km
2 miles	
3 miles	
4 miles	
5 miles	

★2 Ben lives 8 miles from his school. Approximately how far is this in km?

A1 Lesley wrote these statements.
Copy the table.
Put a ✔ in either the true or the false column.

All about me	true	false
My thumb is about 6 cm long.		
My hand span is about 200 mm wide.		
My ruler is about 30 m long.		
My eraser is about 40 mm long.		
My aunt is about 15.7 m tall.		
I live about 40 km from school.		

A2 3 snails took part in a race.
They crawled these distances in 10 minutes.

Change all the measurements to millimetres.

Hector   3000 mm
Hamish   316 cm
Hugo   3.2 m

a Which snail won?

b What was the winning distance in millimetres?

B1 The Youngs are on a walking holiday in France.
They are walking to a town 50 km away.
On Monday they walk halfway to the town.
On Tuesday they manage half of the remaining distance.

a How many kilometres do they walk in these 2 days?

b How many kilometres have they still to walk?

B2 On Wednesday they walk 8 km. If 1 mile ≈ 1.6 km, about how many miles is that?

B3 Work out how far they must walk to reach the town on Thursday

a in kilometres, **b** in metres,

c to the nearest whole kilometre.

B4 About how many miles must the Young family walk on Thursday?

B5 Altogether the Youngs walk 50 km. About how many miles is that to the nearest mile?

C1

Adrian is training for the 'Run and swim' biathlon.
Each day he has a swim after his run.
Here are his practice distances.

run	swim
4.5 km	250 m
5.25 km	450 m
7.75 km	700 m

Write a training schedule by choosing a different combination of running and swimming distances for each day.
Continue until you have found all the combinations.

Write your answer in 2 ways each time.

DIARY

	run	swim	total
Day 1	4500 m	+ 250 m	= 4750 m or 4.75 km

C2

Mark with a ✗ the days on which Adrian's training schedule is 5 or more miles.

Key idea | A mile is a bit more than 1.5 km. A mile is about 1600 m.

M1.4 Reading scales and rounding lengths

Key idea | You can find the distance between 2 divisions on a scale by counting on or subtracting.

★1 Write the length of each child's standing jump in metres.

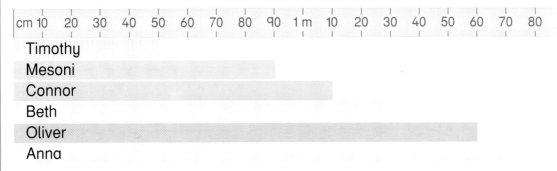

cm 10 20 30 40 50 60 70 80 90 1 m 10 20 30 40 50 60 70 80

Timothy
Mesoni
Connor
Beth
Oliver
Anna

A1 Find the difference in lengths of jump:

   a between Timothy and Mesoni,

   b between Connor and Beth,

   c between Oliver and Anna,

   d between Timothy and Anna.

A2 Which children jumped 2 m to the nearest metre?

A3 The school record is 1.9 m.
Work out how much further each child must jump to equal the school record.

B1 Estimate the length of each object in cm. Now measure and give the answer to the nearest millimetre.
Use the dimension lines ├────┤ to help you.

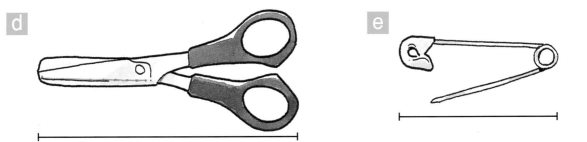

a   b   c

d   e

B2 Look at your answers to B1.

  a For each item work out the total length of a straight line of 10 of them, laid end to end.
  Write each answer in centimetres.

  b Now work out the total lengths of straight lines of 100 of each item.
  Write each answer in metres.

Use your answers to **a** .

B3 You can measure the diameter of the Sports Day medals like this:

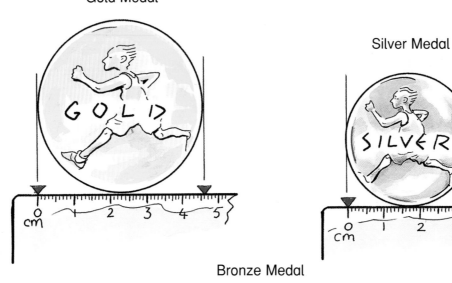

Gold Medal

Silver Medal

Bronze Medal

Give the diameter of each medal to the nearest millimetre.
Write it as a decimal number of centimetres.
Round each measurement to the nearest whole centimetre.
Write your answers in a table like this:

Medal	millimetres	centimetres	nearest centimetre
Gold	☐ mm	☐ . ☐ cm	☐ cm
Silver			
Bronze			

C1 This is the sticker which every competitor gets.

The stickers are sold in strips of 10.
There is a 3 mm gap on either side of each sticker.
How long is a strip of

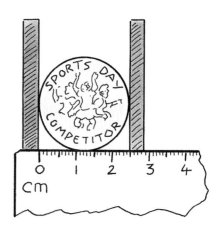

> **a** 10 stickers

> **b** 100 stickers

C2 Estimate how many stickers are in a strip which is:

> **a** 1 metre long

> **b** 10 metres long

Show how you worked out your answers.

C3 What is the greatest number of stickers that can be cut from an A4 sheet?

Key idea You can find the distance between 2 divisions on a scale by counting on or subtracting.

M 2.1 Using standard masses

★1 Total these masses.

★2 Write these masses in grams.

a 1 kg   b 3 kg   c 5 kg   d $\frac{1}{2}$ kg   e $\frac{1}{4}$ kg   f $\frac{3}{4}$ kg

A1 List the masses in order from heaviest to lightest.
Write the total mass of each set.

A2 Write these masses in grams.

a 4 kg   b $1\frac{1}{4}$ kg   c $1\frac{1}{2}$ kg

d $1\frac{3}{4}$ kg   e 2.5 kg   f $\frac{1}{10}$ kg

A3 Write these masses in kilograms and grams.

a 7260 g   b 7060 g   c 7200 g

d 4050 g   e 4900 g   f 4950 g

B1 Use 10 g, 20 g, 50 g, 100 g, 200 g, 500 g and 1 kg masses.
Balance each parcel using the fewest masses possible. Write down the masses you use.

a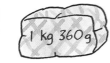

b

c

d

e

f

B2 Write these masses in grams.

a $\frac{3}{10}$ kg

b $\frac{7}{10}$ kg

c $1\frac{1}{10}$ kg

d $\frac{1}{100}$ kg

e $\frac{5}{100}$ kg

f 2.25 kg

B3 a Work out the mass of the bag of oranges.

b Work out the approximate mass of 1 orange.

C1 You have only 50 g, 100 g and 200 g masses. Write all the combinations of masses that you could use to balance a parcel weighing 500 g.

C2 You have only 100 g, 200 g and 500 g masses. Write all the combinations of masses that you could use to balance a parcel weighing 1 kg.

Key idea When totalling the standard masses used to balance an object, begin with the heaviest.

M 2.2 Reading scales

★1 These kitchen scales show 2 kg 300 g.

What masses do these scales show?

a  b 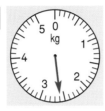 c  d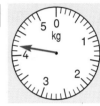

e  f  g  h

A1 What masses do these scales show?

a 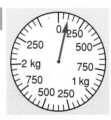 b 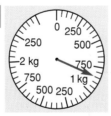 c  d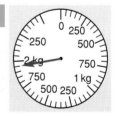

A2 Use CM 4.
Draw arrows to show these masses.

a $3\frac{1}{4}$ kg and $2\frac{1}{2}$ kg on scale a

b 500 g, $1\frac{3}{4}$ kg and 5 kg 500 g on scale b

c 600 g and 1 kg 100 g on scale c

d $\frac{1}{2}$ kg and 1 kg 500 g on scale d

B1 What masses do these scales show?

 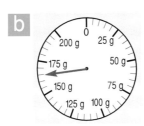 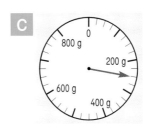 

B2 Use CM 4.

Draw arrows to show these masses.

a   600 g and 850 g on scale e

b   1 kg 250 g and $\frac{3}{4}$ kg on scale f

c   135 g and $\frac{1}{4}$ kg on scale g

d   260 g and 105 g on scale h

e   50 g and 325 g on scale i

C1 You need kitchen scales and ten 2p coins.

a   Work out the mass of one hundred 2p coins.

b   Approximately how many 2p coins would balance 1 kg?

c   Approximately how many 2p coins would
balance a person who weighs 55 kg?
What would be the total value of the coins?

You could use a
calculator to help you, but
show your working.

Key idea   Use the number of intervals on a scale to work out the value of each one.

M 2.3 Rounding decimal measurements

Use what you know about decimals to round masses to the nearest whole kilogram.

A1 Round each mass to the nearest whole kilogram.

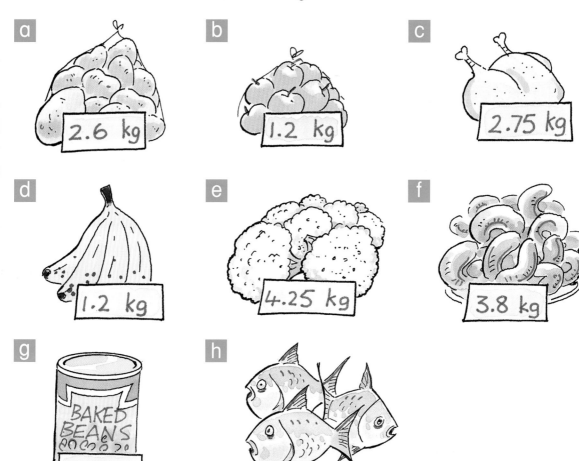

a 2.6 kg

b 1.2 kg

c 2.75 kg

d 1.2 kg

e 4.25 kg

f 3.8 kg

g BAKED BEANS 2.5 kg

h 0.4 kg

B1 Write each answer as kilograms. What is the mass of

a 3 jars of coffee?

b 4 bags of flour?

c 4 packets of salt?

d $\frac{1}{2}$ a tub of margarine?

e   1 packet of tea and 1 bag of flour?

f   1 bag of sugar and 1 packet of salt?

g   3 bags of flour and 2 jars of coffee?

h   6 tubs of margarine, 4 packets of tea and 2 packets of stock cubes?

Example

tea 100 g = 0.1 kg

coffee 250 g = 0.25 kg

350 g = 0.35 kg

B2   What is the difference in mass between

a the flour and coffee?   **b** the coffee and stock cubes?   **c** the margarine and tea?

B3   Make up 2 more problems of your own to answer.

B4   Round your answers to B1 to the nearest whole kilogram.

C1   Look at the masses of the food items above.
How many ways can you make 1 kg?
You can use each mass more than once.

C2   The combined mass of the triplets is 21.6 kg.
Andrew is 400 g lighter than Bobby.
Bobby is 0.2 kg heavier then Colin.
Find the mass of each baby.

Key idea | Use what you know about decimals to round masses to the nearest whole kilogram.

M 2.4 Cook book problems

Key idea	Use what you know about numbers to solve problems involving mass.

★1 What is the total mass of

a the walnuts and the Greek yogurt?

b the pasta, the bacon and the blue cheese?

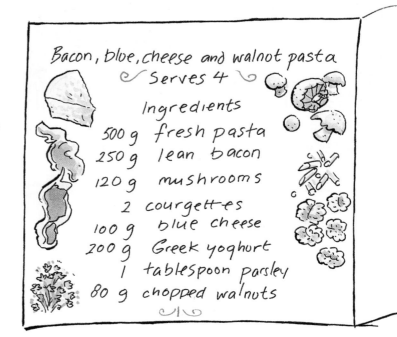

Bacon, blue, cheese and walnut pasta
Serves 4
Ingredients
500 g fresh pasta
250 g lean bacon
120 g mushrooms
2 courgettes
100 g blue cheese
200 g Greek yoghurt
1 tablespoon parsley
80 g chopped walnuts

★2 What is the difference in mass between

a the blue cheese and the walnuts?

b the Greek yogurt and the blue cheese?

★3 The recipe above is for 4 people.
What mass of each of the following ingredients would you need for 8 people:

a Greek yogurt?　　b pasta?　　c bacon?

★4 A courgette weighs about 200 grams.
Approximately how many courgettes would you get in a kilogram?

A1 What is the total mass of

a the bacon, the blue cheese, the Greek yogurt and the walnuts?

b the walnuts, the mushrooms and the bacon?

A2 You buy two 125 g cartons of yogurt and you use 200 g for the recipe.
How much yogurt is left over?

A3   You have a 250 g packet of chopped walnuts. You use the recipe 3 times.
What mass of walnuts do you have left?

A4   The recipe opposite is for 4 people.

Adapt the recipe for   a   2 people   b   6 people.

List all the ingredients and the quantities needed.

You could use a calculator to check your answers to these questions.

B1   Look at the pasta recipe on the opposite page.

If <u>each</u> courgette weighs 200 g and the parsley weighs 5 g, what is the total mass of all the ingredients in the recipe for 4 people?

B2   You need 500 g of pasta for the recipe.
You use up 220 g from an old packet.
You take the rest from a new 1 kg packet.
How much is left in the new packet?

B3   The recipe opposite is for 4 people.

Adapt the recipe for   a   1 person   b   5 people.

List all the ingredients and the quantity needed.

B4   Bacon costs £6 per kilogram, pasta costs £1.50 per kilogram and blue cheese costs £3 per half-kilogram.
What is the total cost of these ingredients in the recipe for 4 people?

C1   What is the total mass of the uncooked pasta dish for 4 people to the nearest kilogram?

Use your answer to B1.

C2   Calculate the mass of

a   the pasta   b   the bacon

as a fraction of the rounded mass of the whole dish.

Key idea | Use what you know about numbers to solve problems involving mass.

Using standard capacities

Key idea	$\frac{1}{10}$ litre = 100 ml and $\frac{1}{100}$ litre = 10 ml.

A1 Write these capacities in litres and millilitres.

a 4750 ml   b 4700 ml   c 4070 ml   d 4007 ml   e 4570 ml

A2 Write these capacities in millilitres.

a $2\frac{1}{2}$ litres   b $5\frac{1}{4}$ litres   c $1\frac{1}{10}$ litres   d $6\frac{3}{4}$ litres   e $8\frac{1}{10}$ litres

A3 John filled these jugs with fruit juice.
Work out how much juice is in each jug.

a

500 ml + 250 ml + 100 ml + 50 ml

b

500 ml + 100 ml + 100 ml + 50 ml + 10 ml

c

250 ml + 100 ml + 100 ml + 10 ml + 10 ml

d

500 ml + 250 ml + 100 ml + 10 ml

e

250 ml + 50 ml + 10 ml + 10 ml + 10 ml

B1

Fill each container using the least number of standard measures.
Record the measures you use.

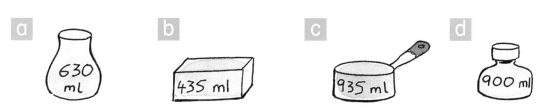

a   630 mL   b   435 ml   c   935 ml   d   900 ml

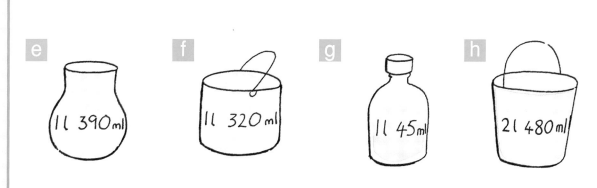

e   1 l 390 ml   f   1 l 320 ml   g   1 l 45 ml   h   2 l 480 ml

B2 You have these measuring jugs and an empty container.

Find a way to pour 1 litre of water into the empty container using

a   2 measures,

b   3 measures,

c   4 measures,

d   5 measures,

e   6 measures.

Example
500 ml + 500 ml = 1 litre

B3 Tom estimated then measured the capacity of 5 containers with these measuring jugs.

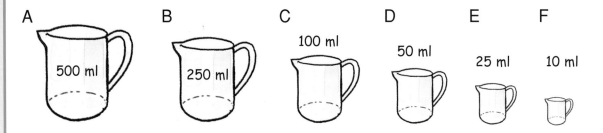

A 500 ml B 250 ml C 100 ml D 50 ml E 25 ml F 10 ml

For each container, work out the difference in millilitres between the estimated and measured capacity.

Container	Estimate	Jugs used
a jar	$\frac{3}{4}$ l	1 of A + 3 of B + 2 of F
b vase	1 l	2 of A + 1 of C + 2 of D
c bottle	$\frac{1}{2}$ l	5 of D + 5 of E
d bowl	$1\frac{1}{4}$ l	2 of A + 3 of D + 4 of F
e pan	1 l 500 ml	4 of B + 3 of C + 1 of E + 2 of F

C1 You have 4 containers
of paint and an empty paint tin.

red + blue = purple
blue + yellow = green
red + yellow = orange

 Red 10 ml  Blue 25 ml  Yellow 50 ml  White 100 ml

You can make different shades of paint when you pour 2 or more of the containers of paint into the empty tin.

Example: 10 ml red + 100 ml white = 110 ml vibrant pink

Make 10 different shades of paint.
Give each shade a name and write the amount in millilitres.

Key idea	$\frac{1}{10}$ litre = 100 ml and $\frac{1}{100}$ litre = 10 ml.

Reading scales

| **Key idea** | Use the number of intervals on a scale to work out the value of each one. |

A1 You need CM 7 and coloured pens.

Draw a straight line to show the level
of the liquid, then colour the liquid up
to the level.

a   400 ml in jug 1

b   340 ml in jug 2

c   150 ml in cylinder 3

d   280 ml in cylinder 4

e   70 ml in jug 5

f   38 ml in cylinder 6

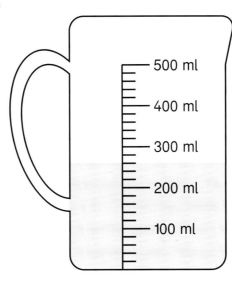

260 ml

A2 Mark the new levels when you pour

a   40 ml of water into containers 2 and 4,

b   50 ml of water into containers 1 and 3.

A3 Mark the new levels when you pour

a   30 ml out of jug 5,

b   10 ml out of cylinder 6.

B1 Work out how much water you need to add to each jug to raise the level to the 1 litre mark.

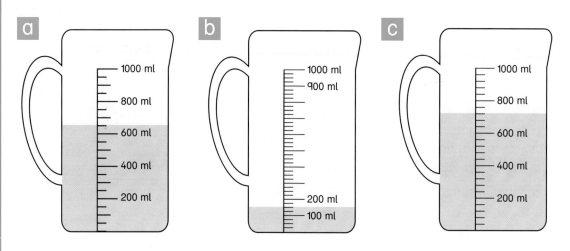

B2 Work out how many millilitres of water you need to add to each container to raise the level to 500 ml.

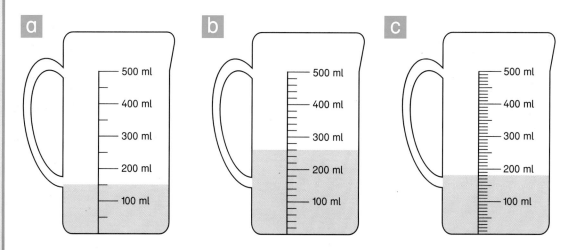

B3   Aunt Sophie's Secret Squash Recipe

Take 240 ml of freshly squeezed orange juice and half this quantity of freshly squeezed lime juice.
Add ice-cold spring water. (You need twice as much water as orange.)
Stir together.

Draw a jug and mark it with a suitable scale.
Draw a straight line to show the level of the liquid when you make up Aunt Sophie's recipe.

C1   Baby Joe drinks milk from a bottle 5 times a day.
At the beginning of each feed the bottle contains 250 ml of warm milk.
The pictures show how much milk was left in the bottle at the end of each feed on Tuesday.

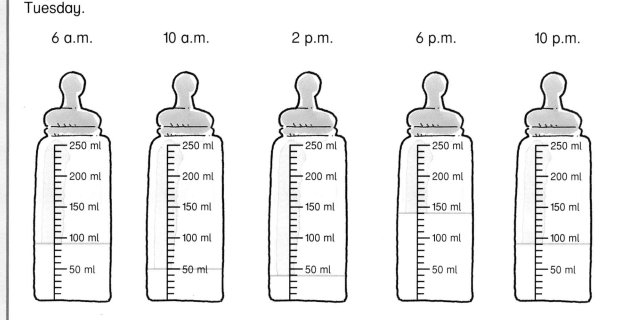

| 6 a.m. | 10 a.m. | 2 p.m. | 6 p.m. | 10 p.m. |

Work out how much milk Joe drank altogether on Tuesday.

Key idea   Use the number of intervals on a scale to work out the value of each one.

M 3.3 Rounding decimal measurements

Key idea	You can use what you know about decimals to round capacities to the nearest litre.

A1 Write each amount as a decimal number of litres, e.g. 2 l 300 ml = 2.3 l

a 1 l 200 ml   b 2 l 500 ml   c 400 ml   d 4 l 250 ml

e 1 l 750 ml   f 1 l 500 ml   g 3 l 200 ml   h 4 l 100 ml

A2 Round each of your answers from A1 to the nearest litre.

B1 The children are having a party.

Write your answers to these questions in decimal form.

a How much more cola does Anil's glass hold than Zak's?

b How much cola is there altogether in Zak's glass and Emma's glass?

c Zak pours himself 2 full glasses of cola from a new 1 litre bottle. How much cola is left in the bottle?

B2 How many times could Emma fill her glass from a full bottle of cola?

B3

   a Round the capacity of each child's glass to nearest 100 ml.

   b Add the rounded amounts to find out roughly how much cola would be needed to fill all the glasses.

   c Now add the actual amounts to see how close the rounded estimate was.

   d Find the difference between the totals for **b** and **c** .

B4

Miss Smith is buying the soft drinks for the Year 5 party.
The paper cups they will use hold 300 ml.

Each of the 30 children can have 2 drinks.
How many litres of drink should she buy?

C1

Your group needs:
a clear, unmarked plastic bottle or jar; large buttons or marbles; funnel; water; measuring cylinder.

You have a jar of sliced beetroot (buttons) or olives (marbles).
The beetroot or olives are kept in vinegar or oil (water) to preserve them.

Measure the amount of vinegar or oil you need to add to the jar to
cover the food and still leave space of about 1 cm at the top of the jar.

C2

What if ... you had another jar which is double the capacity of the first?
Is the amount of liquid needed to cover the beetroot (or olives) doubled?
Investigate.

C3

Use your results from C1.
Work out how much liquid the bottling plant at the factory would use for

   a 100 identical jars of beetroot or olives,

   b 1000 identical jars.

> **Key idea** | You can use what you know about decimals to round capacities to the nearest litre.

M 3.4 Metric and imperial units

Key idea	A pint is a bit more than half a litre. A gallon is a bit less than 5 litres.

★1 Write the unit, pints or gallons, you would use to measure the capacity of these farm objects.

a

b

c

d MILK CHURN

e

f DAIRY

I pint is slightly more than ½ litre
I pint is approximately equal to 570 ml
I gallon is slightly less than 5 litres
8 pints is the same as I gallon

I pint > ½ litre
I pint ≈ 570 ml
I gallon < 5 litres
8 pints = I gallon

A1 Copy and complete. Write the correct symbol, < or >, to make these statements true.

a 1 pint ☐ 500 ml

b 1 pint ☐ 1 l

c 1 gallon ☐ 5700 ml

d 8 pints ☐ 5 l

A2 Copy each sentence and write whether it is true or false.

a 1 pint ≈ 570 ml

b 5 l > 1 gallon

c 1 pint < 0.5 l

d 8 pints = 1 gallon

e 1 pint > $\frac{1}{2}$ l

f 5 l > 8 pints

g 10 pints ≈ 5700 ml

h 50 l < 10 gallons

A3 The Roberts family have 4 pints of milk delivered each day except Sunday.

a How many pints are delivered in a week?

b How many gallons is that?

B1 The bottles show how much milk each lamb gets per feed.

LIZ 150 ml
LARRY 170 ml
LENA 190 ml
LOLLY 250 ml
LOGAN 380 ml

a Which 3 bottles can be filled exactly, leaving no milk in the jug?

1 pint 570 ml

b How many pints of milk are used to give all the lambs a feed?

c For how many feeds will 1 gallon of milk last?

d Lena is fed 6 times a day. How many pints does she drink?

e How many more millilitres of milk does Lolly get than Liz in 6 feeds?

f Which lamb drinks 4 pints in 6 feeds?

B2 A farm tractor travels 25 miles to the gallon.

a How many gallons does it need for 100 miles of farm work?

b Approximately how many litres will it use for

   • 100 miles?   • 250 miles?

C1

You need 5 mm graph paper.

a Copy and complete this table.

pints	millilitres	litres
1 pint	570 ml	0.57 l
2 pints		
4 pints		
8 pints		

b Construct a line graph to show the relationship between pints and litres.

C2 Use your graph to answer these questions.

a About how many pints are equal to

- 4 litres?
- 2 litres?

b How many litres are approximately equal to

- 3.5 pints?
- 4.5 pints?
- 7 pints?

C3 Use the table to work out the answers to these questions.

a What is 16 pints to the nearest litre?

b How many pints are approximately equal to 45 litres?

Key idea A pint is a bit more than half a litre. A gallon is a bit less than 5 litres.

Perimeters of polygons

| Key idea | The perimeter of a regular polygon is length of side x number of sides. |

★1 Find the perimeter of these rectangles.

Rectangle	Perimeter
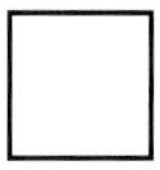 □	4 cm
a	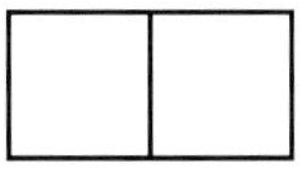
b	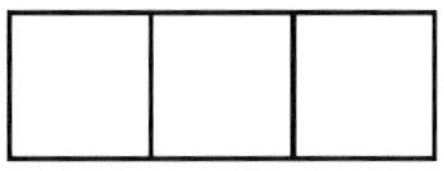
c	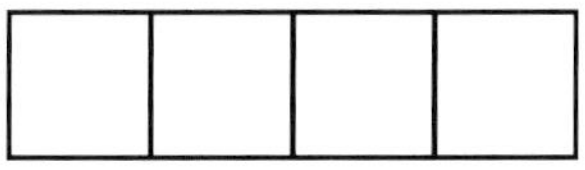
d	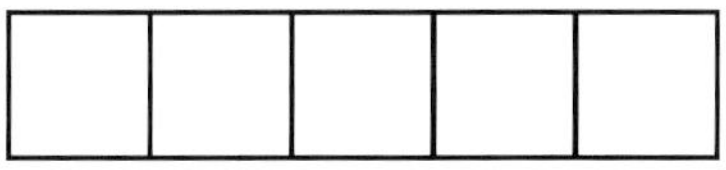

A1 You need a ruler.
Find the perimeter of each shape in centimetres.
Write how you worked it out.

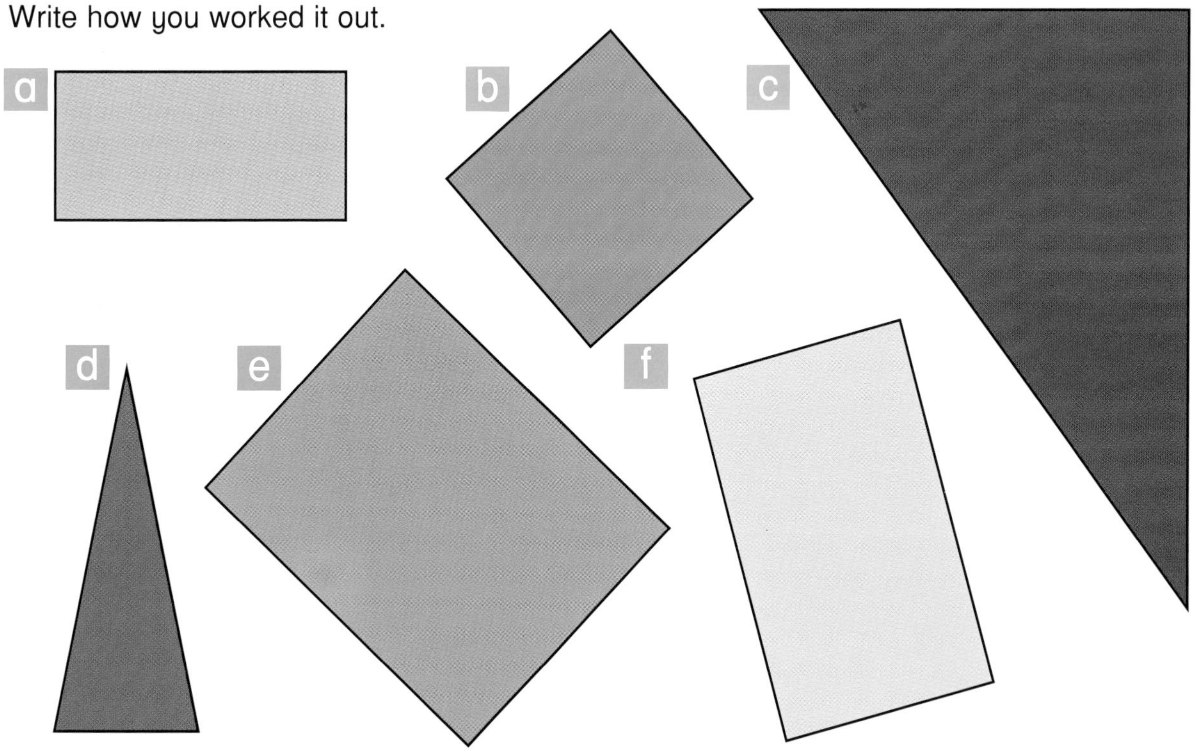

a

b

c

d

e

f

A2 Find the difference between the longest and shortest perimeter.

B1 You need a ruler.
Find the perimeter of these regular polygons.
Measure the sides to the nearest millimetre.

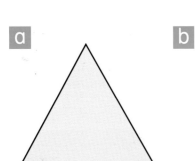

a

b

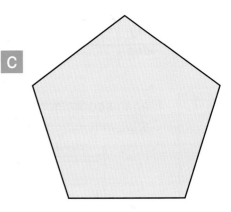

c

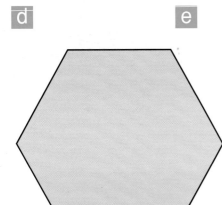

d

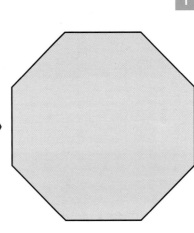

e

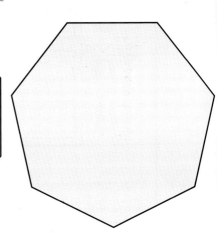

f

B2 Work out the perimeter of a regular 10-sided shape.
Copy and complete the table.

Length of side in cm	1	2	3	4	5	6	7	8	9	10
Perimeter in cm										

B3 You need centimetre squared paper.

Make a table.

a Construct the next 2 rectangles in this pattern.

b Calculate the perimeter of all 6 rectangles.

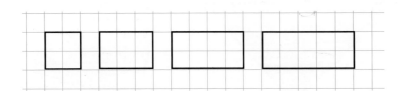

| Key idea | The perimeter of a regular polygon is length of side x number of sides. |

M 4.2 The formula for the perimeter of a rectangle

Key idea	The perimeter of a rectangle is twice the length plus twice the breadth, $P = (2 \times l) + (2 \times b)$, or the length plus the breadth doubled, $P = 2 \times (l + b)$.

★1 If each square has sides of 1 cm, calculate the perimeter of each stamp.
Show, with jottings, how you found the answer.

A1 You need centimetre squared paper.
Copy and complete these rectangles.
Calculate the perimeter of each one.

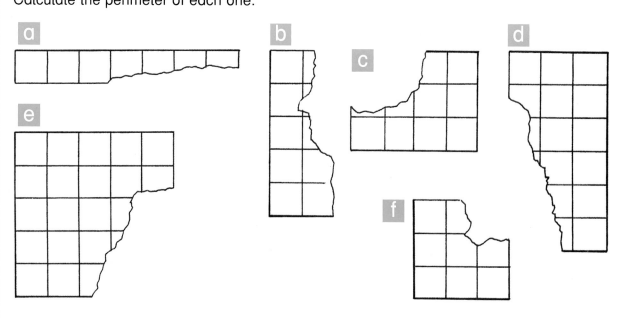

B1 | Use a formula to calculate these perimeters.

Example

4 cm

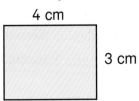

3 cm

(2 x 4 cm) + (2 x 3 cm) = 8 cm + 6 cm
= 14 cm

or

2 x (4 cm + 3 cm) = 2 x 7 cm
= 14 cm

4 cm

a

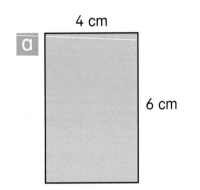

6 cm

5 cm

b

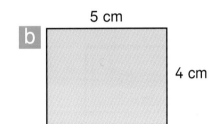

4 cm

7 cm

c

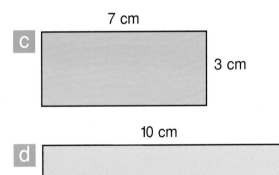

3 cm

5 cm

e

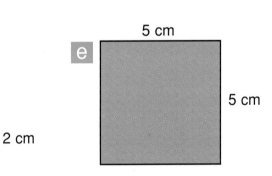

5 cm

10 cm

d

2 cm

B2 | You need centimetre squared paper.
This is part of a rectangle with a
perimeter of 22 cm.
Construct 3 different rectangles
each with a perimeter of 22 cm.

B3 | Construct 3 different rectangles each with a perimeter of 24 cm.

B4 | 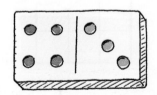 This domino has a perimeter of 30 cm.
One side measures 5 cm.
Find the length of the other side.

C1

You need centimetre squared paper.
You have 12 square tiles with sides of 2 cm.
Use all 12 tiles to construct

a   the rectangle with the greatest perimeter,

b   the rectangle with the smallest perimeter.

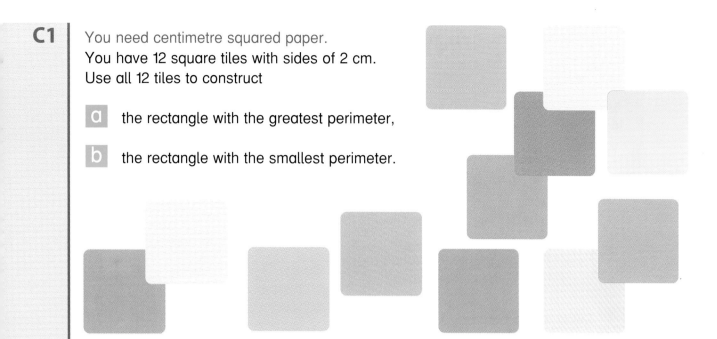

c   What happens if you repeat the activity using only 11 tiles? 10 tiles? 9 tiles?

Discuss your findings with your teacher.

Key idea   The perimeter of a rectangle is twice the length plus twice the breadth,
$P = (2 \times l) + (2 \times b)$, or the length plus the breadth doubled, $P = 2 \times (l + b)$.

M 4.3 Calculating areas

Key idea | Area is measured in square units. The area of a rectangle can be found by multiplying its length by its breadth.

★1   You need 1 cm square tiles.

    a   Make 3 different rectangles.

    b   Count the tiles you use for each rectangle.
Write its area in square centimetres.

    c   Swap with a partner.
Find the area of their rectangles.

Example

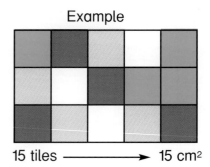

15 tiles ⟶ 15 cm²

A1   Find the area of rectangles P, Q and R.

Example

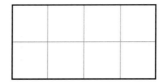

2 rows of 4 square centimetres
area = 8 cm²

Q
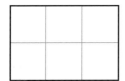

P
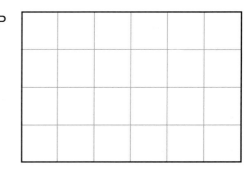

R
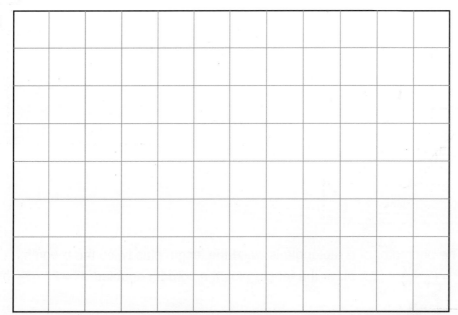

A2

a   Write the length and breath of rectangle P.

b   Draw these rectangles on 1 cm squared paper.

   • Add 1 cm to the sides of P
   • Add 3 cm to the sides of P
   • Add 4 cm to the sides of P

c   Find the area of each rectangle you have drawn.

B1   Copy and complete the table for these rectangles:

rectangle	length in cm	breadth in cm	area in cm²
a	☐ cm	☐ cm	☐ cm²
b			
c			
d			
e			
f			

a

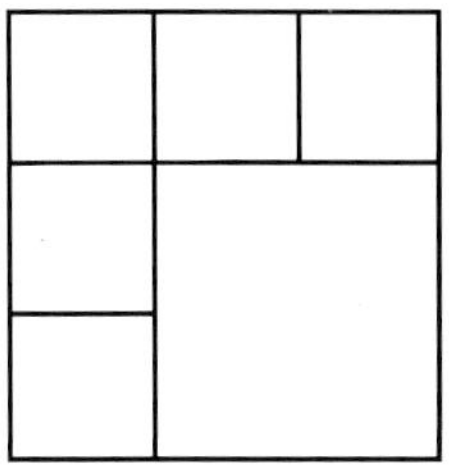

b

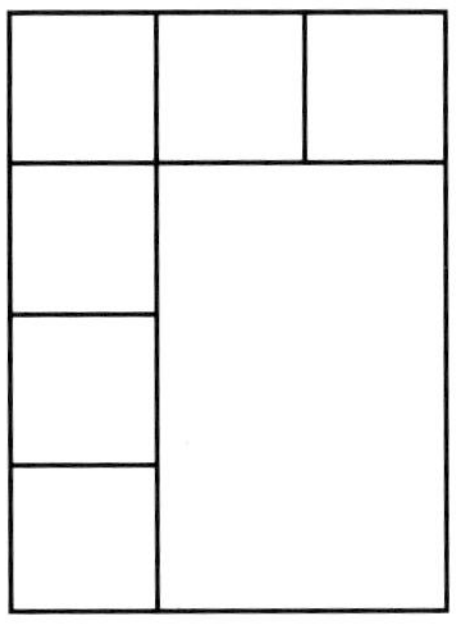

c

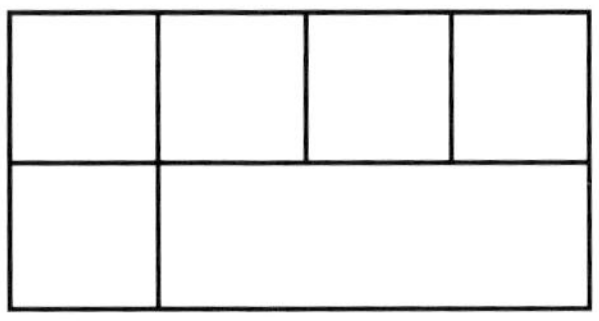

d

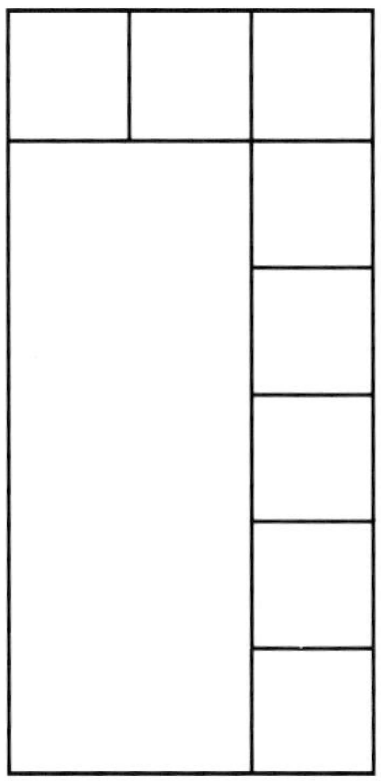

e

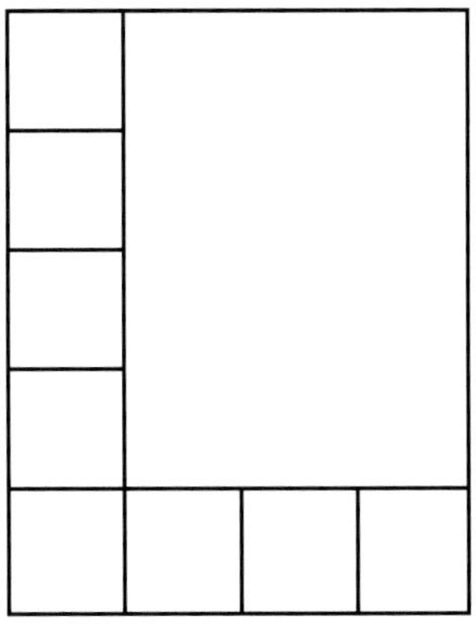

f

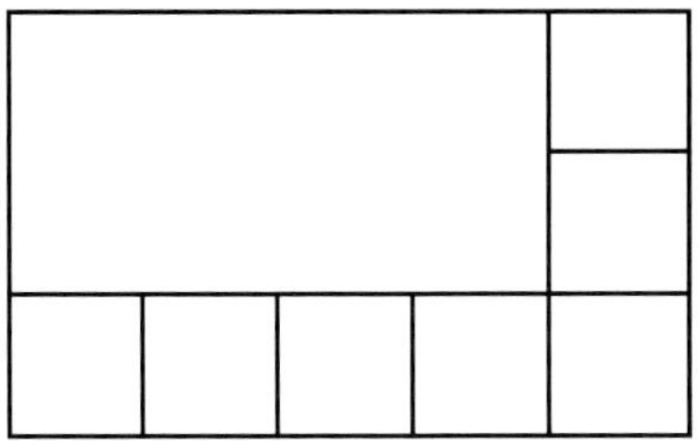

B2

a Work out the area of each advertisement.

b List them in order. Begin with the largest.

Example

4 cm

3 cm

area = length x breadth
= 4 cm x 3 cm
= 12 cm²

Key idea	Area is measured in square units. The area of a rectangle can be found by multiplying its length by its breadth.

M 4.4   Using a formula to calculate the area of a rectangle

Key idea | You can use the formula 'area = length x breadth' to find the area of a rectangle.

A1 Which size of square would you choose for measuring these areas: mm², cm² or m²

	Size of square
1 mm²	1 square millimetre
1 cm²	1 square centimetre
1 m²	1 square metre

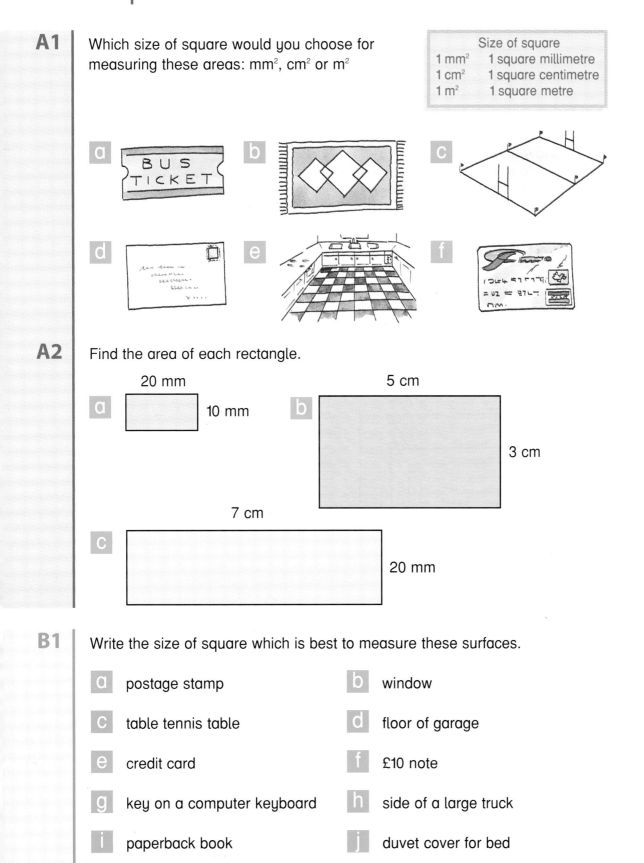

a   BUS TICKET

b

c

d

e

f

A2 Find the area of each rectangle.

a   20 mm   10 mm

b   5 cm   3 cm

c   7 cm   20 mm

B1 Write the size of square which is best to measure these surfaces.

a   postage stamp

b   window

c   table tennis table

d   floor of garage

e   credit card

f   £10 note

g   key on a computer keyboard

h   side of a large truck

i   paperback book

j   duvet cover for bed

B2   Work out the area of each of these.

a
60 mm

40 mm

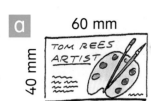

b
20 cm

20 cm

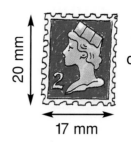

20 mm

17 mm

Example
area = length x breadth
= 20 mm x 17 mm
= 340 cm²

c
40 cm

40 cm

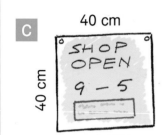

d
25 m

10 m

e
60 cm

90 cm

B3

3 cm

3 cm

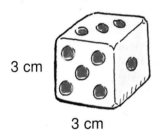

a   Find the area of one dice face.

b   Work out the total area of all 6 faces.

C1

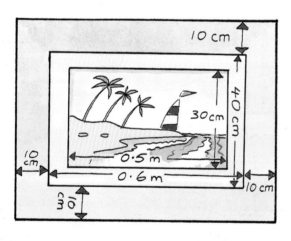

10 cm

40 cm

30 cm

0.5 m

0.6 m

10 cm

10 cm

10 cm

a   Calculate the area of the picture in cm².

b   Find a way to work out the perimeter of the framed picture.

c   Calculate the area of wall covered by the picture and its frame.

Key idea | You can use the formula 'area = length x breadth' to find the area of a rectangle.

M 5.1 Reading clocks

A1 Write these times as 24-hour clock times.

Add 12 to the p.m. time to find the 24-hour time.

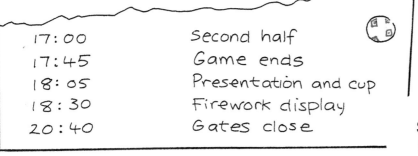

half past 2   Gates open
quarter past 3   Marching band and singing
quarter to 4   National anthems
4 o'clock   Kick-off
quarter to 5   Half time

A2 Write these times as 12-hour digital clock times.

17:00   Second half
17:45   Game ends
18:05   Presentation and cup
18:30   Firework display
20:40   Gates close

Subtract 12 from the 24-hour time to find the p.m. time.

B1 These clocks show 24-hour times.

For some of the digital times the analogue clock will look the same.

Example

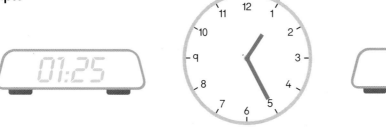

01:25   13.25

Find pairs of these digital times that would look the same on an analogue clock.

02:35   19:10   07:10   00:35
16:10
12:35   23:20   12:23   04:10
10:20   20:20   11:20

B2 Copy and complete this table.

Time	12-hour clock	24-hour clock
6 o'clock in the evening	6:00 p.m.	18:00
quarter past 8 in the morning		
	3:23 p.m.	
		16:20
12 minutes past 2 in the afternoon		
	9:20 a.m.	
		17:45
10 to 7 in the morning		
	11:55 a.m.	
5 past midnight		

C1 You have a 6-hour long-play video tape.

You set it to record these programmes.

Copy and complete the table.

Day	Programme	Start time	Finish time	Duration
Mon	Walking with Dinosaurs	20:35		60 min
Tue	Record Breakers	17:10		25 min
Wed	National Lottery		20:15	40 min
Thur	Adventures of Robin Hood	21:25	23:05	
Fri	Toy Story		19:45	85 min

C2 Now work out how many minutes
of recording time are left on the tape.

Key idea	If you add 12 to the p.m. time, you can find the 24-hour clock time.

M 5.2 Solving problems: clocks and units of time

Key idea	You can use what you know about time to solve problems.

★1   Look at these start and stop times for a video recorder.

Work out how long each recording lasts.

Copy and complete the table.

Start	Stop	Recording time
17:15	18:00	45 min
20:10	21:00	
16:20	17:00	
22:40	23:00	
13:35	14:00	
15:12	16:00	
11:25	12:00	

★2   Copy and complete this sentence.

I worked out the recording time by ...

A1   A coach leaves school at 09:45 and arrives in London at 11:00.

How long did the journey take?

A2   A Grand Prix race ended at 16:20. The race lasted for 95 minutes.

At what time did the race begin?

A3   Ben's walk to school takes 8.5 minutes.

How much time does he take walking to and from school

   in one day?   b   in a school week?

A4   Kerry went to bed at 21:30.

Her alarm went off at 07:15 the next day.

How long was she in bed?

A5   Bill is having his birthday party at the Leisure Centre.

The party lasts for $2\frac{1}{4}$ hours.

How much time will they have for eating?

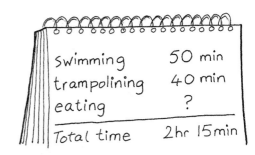

swimming	50 min
trampolining	40 min
eating	?
Total time	2hr 15min

A team of 6 parents at Mill Street Primary entered a mini-marathon event.

The table shows their individual times and their previous personal best times.

Entrant	Time taken		Previous personal best time	
	hr	min	hr	min
Tina	1	56	2	05
Danielle	2	11	2	22
Ross	1	49	2	02
David	1	58	2	17
Anna	2	02	2	05
Duncan	1	55	2	10

B1   Write the names in order, starting with the fastest time.

B2   What was the time difference between the fastest and slowest team members?

B3   Which two team members were closest in time?

B4   Which team member most improved their personal best on the day?

B5   Work out the combined times for

   a   Danielle and Ross,

   b   David and Anna,

   c   the whole team.

B6   The winning team had a total time of 11 hours 45 minutes.

   If Anna had improved her personal best by another 5 minutes, would the parents at Mill Street Primary have won the event?

C1   Work with a partner.

   Draw up an imaginary TV guide of 5 of your favourite programmes for the perfect evening's viewing.

   Make up some problems about your guide.

   Swap your programme with another pair and solve their problems.

| Key idea | You can use what you know about time to solve problems. |

M 5.4 Solving problems: timetables and units of time

| Key idea | You can use what you know about time to solve problems. |

	A	B	C
London	11:15	13:20	15:30
Oxford	13:05	15:00	17:10
Birmingham	14:30	16:15	18:50
Manchester	17:00	19:30	21:15

Use this timetable to answer the questions.

★1   How long does coach A take to get from London to Manchester?

★2   a   When does the 14:30 from Birmingham reach Manchester?

     b   How long does the journey take?

★3   If you need to be in Oxford by 16:00, which is the best coach to catch in London?

★4   If you arrive at Birmingham at 14:50, how long must you wait for the next coach to Manchester?

★5   How long does coach C take from London to Oxford.

SS1.1 Describing rectangles

> **Key idea** | A rectangle has 4 right angles, its opposite sides are equal and its diagonals bisect one another.

A1 You need scissors, glue and CM 15.

  a Cut out the shapes and sort them into 'rectangles' and 'not rectangles'.

  b Glue them into your book in their 2 labelled groups.

B1 You need scissors, a ruler, a large sheet of paper, glue and a copy of CM 15.

  a Cut out the 2-D shapes.

  b Draw the diagonals on the shapes, using a ruler.

  Tick any shapes where the diagonals bisect each other.

  Example

  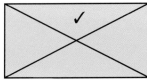

  c Draw a Carroll diagram with labels 'rectangles' and 'not rectangles', 'diagonals bisect each other' and 'diagonals do not bisect each other'.

  d Glue your shapes in the correct places on the diagram.

  e Write down what you notice.

C1 You need some dotty square grid paper.

Draw some quadrilaterals of your own to test if your findings are still true.

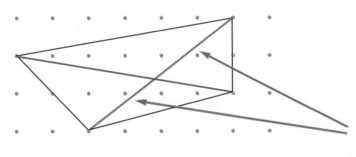

You might need to measure these to compare them.

Reasoning about rectangles

| **Key idea** | You can use what you know about rectangles to investigate and explain patterns. |

A1 | 12 square challenge

You need square tiles, squared paper and a partner.

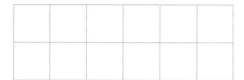 This rectangle is made with 12 squares.

a Arrange 12 squares to make a different rectangle.

Check that you have not made the same rectangle and simply turned it round.

b Find how many different rectangles you can make with 12 squares.
Record your findings on squared paper to present to the class.

B1 | 5 rectangle challenge

You need squared paper, square tiles and a partner.

How many square tiles are needed to make exactly 5 different rectangles?

Work with a partner and record your findings on squared paper.

B2 | Write a description of how you solved this puzzle.

C1

This is a 3 x 3 grid.
2 different rectangles have already been identified inside the grid.

How many different rectangles can you find altogether in a 3 x 3 grid?

Draw the different rectangles.

SS 1.3 Classifying triangles 1

| **Key idea** | Triangles can be classified by looking at their sides and angles. |

A1 You need CM 16, scissors and large sheets of paper.

Cut out triangles a, b, c, d, e and f.

Draw a large copy of this Venn diagram.

Use the diagram to sort your triangles.

Draw round the triangles and label each drawing with its letter to record your work.

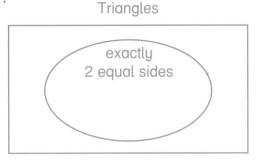

A2 Draw a new Venn diagram and sort the triangles again.

Draw round the triangles and letter them to record your work.

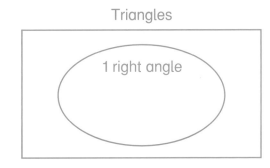

B1 You need triangles cut from CM 16 and large sheets of paper.

Make a large copy of this Venn diagram and use it to sort your triangles.

Draw round the triangles and label each drawing with its letter to record your work.

Can an isosceles triangle have a right angle?

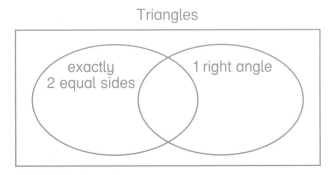

B2 Draw a new Venn diagram, changing the labels to 'scalene' and 'right-angled'.

Sort the triangles again, and record them by drawing and lettering.

Can you find a triangle that is both scalene and right-angled?

C1 Draw a large copy of this diagram:

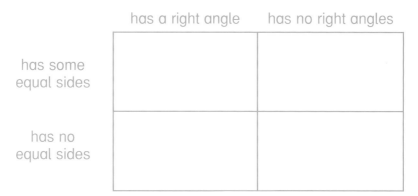

Think about each section of the diagram in turn.

If you think there is a triangle with these properties, draw it and write its name.

If you think it is not possible to have a triangle in any section, leave it blank.

Key idea | Triangles can be classified by looking at their sides and angles.

SS 1.4 Classifying triangles 2

Key idea	When you know the type of triangle, you know how many lines of symmetry it has.

A1 You need CM 16.

Label each triangle equilateral, isosceles or scalene.

A2 Cut out the triangles.

Choose one of each type and fold it to find how many lines of symmetry it has.

Will other triangles of each type have the same number of lines of symmetry?

B1 You need triangles cut from CM 16.

   a Sort the triangles into 3 groups, equilateral, isosceles and scalene.

   b Take each group of triangles in turn. Mark all the lines of symmetry.

   c What do you notice about the number of lines of symmetry in each group?

B2 Try a few triangles of your own to check your findings.

C1

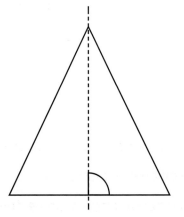

Here is a line of symmetry in a triangle.

What size is the angle where the line of symmetry bisects the base?

Use the triangles from CM 16. Is the angle where a line of symmetry bisects a side always the same?

Write down what you discover.

C2 What else do you notice about lines of symmetry?

Investigating shapes

Key idea	You can use pinboards and dotted grids to investigate triangles and squares.

A1 You need a 3 x 3 pinboard and some elastic bands.

    a Make a triangle like this.

    b Now make some different triangles.

A2 Use CM 17.

Record some of the triangles that you make on a 3 x 3 grid.

A3 Name each of your triangles.

B1 Use CM 17.

Try to draw an isosceles triangle, a scalene triangle, a right-angled triangle and an equilateral triangle on the grids. Are any impossible?

B2 Work with a partner.

How many ways can you find to make triangles of each type? Record your work.

C1 You need a 5 x 5 pinboard, elastic bands and CM 18.

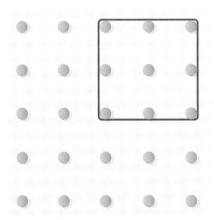

This square is made on a 5 x 5 pinboard.

Find some different squares.

How many different-sized squares can you make altogether on this pinboard?

Record your answers on CM 18.

Think about diagonal lines.

SS 2.1 The octahedron

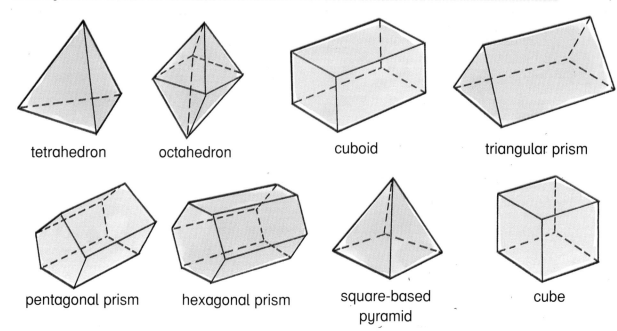

tetrahedron   octahedron   cuboid   triangular prism

pentagonal prism   hexagonal prism   square-based pyramid   cube

A1 Copy and complete this table.

Write the name of each shape above in the correct column.

no faces right-angled	some faces right-angled	all faces right-angled
tetrahedron		

B1 Copy and complete these Venn diagrams.

Write the name of one shape in each region.

a

all faces congruent   at least 1 triangular face

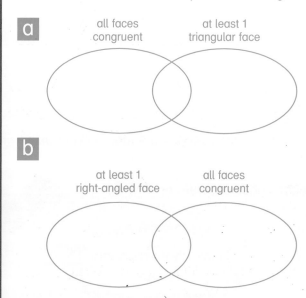

b

at least 1 right-angled face   all faces congruent

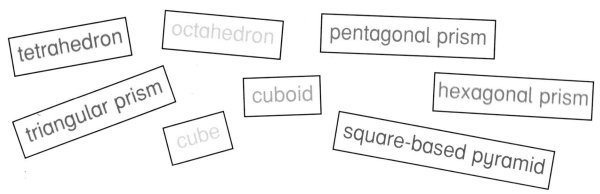

tetrahedron   octahedron   pentagonal prism

triangular prism   cuboid   hexagonal prism

cube   square-based pyramid

B2 Name the 3-D shape being described.

a It has 3 edges meeting at every vertex. All faces are triangular.

b It has 1 right-angled face. The number of edges meeting at one of the vertices is 4.

c It has 3 more edges than a cube. It is a prism.

d It has 6 vertices and both triangular and right-angled faces.

e It has the same number of edges as a cuboid, but it is not a cube.

f It has 8 faces, but not all faces are congruent.

B3 Write 2 facts to describe

a an octahedron,   **b** one of the other 3-D shapes.

C1 You need 1 cm triangular dotty paper.

Draw this net for an octahedron.

• Cut out the net.

• Fold it up to form an octahedron.

• Before you glue the tabs, label the faces 1 to 8 to make a dice.

• Assemble the dice.

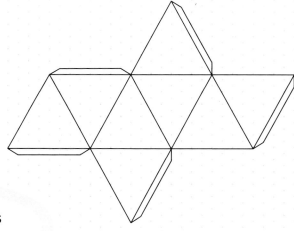

Opposite faces
must add to 9.

Key idea A regular octahedron is a polyhedron with 8 equilateral-triangle faces.

SS2.2 Open cubes

A1 Predict whether each of these pentominoes is a net of an open cube or not.

Record your predictions by copying the table and putting a tick in the 'is a net' or 'is not a net' column.

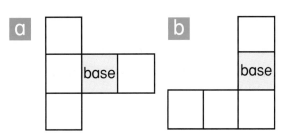

pentomino	prediction		check
	is a net	is not a net	
a	✓		✓
b			
c			
d			
e			
f			
g			
h			

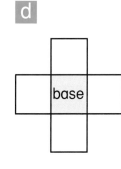

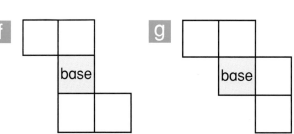

A2 You need interlocking square tiles and Blu-Tack.

Make each pentomino.

Mark the base with Blu-Tack.

Fold up each shape to test your prediction.

Put a tick in the last column of the table if you were correct.

C1   You need 2 cm squared paper and scissors.

This open box has a repeating pattern all the way round.

This is the net of the open box.

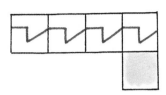

- Copy net a onto squared paper.
- Decide where the repeating pattern will be and draw it on the net.
- Cut out the net and fold it up to check that the pattern repeats at the same level all the way round the open cube.
- Repeat for nets b to f.
- Stick each net in your book.

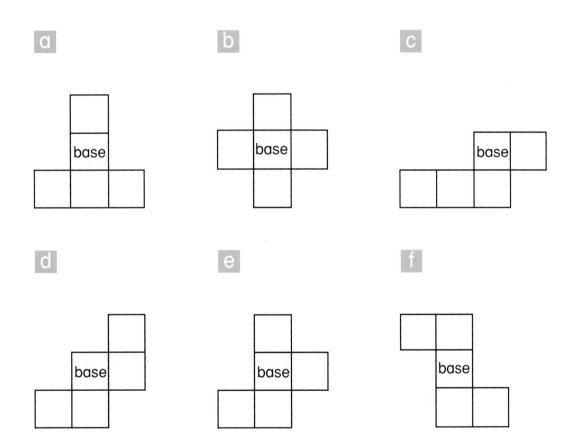

Key idea   Some pentominoes are nets that form an open cube.

SS 2.3 Visualising 3-D shapes

> **Key idea** | Use the clues in the incomplete shape to help you visualise the cuboid.

A1 Work with a partner. You need a supply of interlocking cubes in 2 colours.

Rules

Each player builds a shape using interlocking cubes of one colour.

In turn, each player says the least number of cubes needed to turn their partner's shape into a cuboid. Use cubes of a different colour to complete the cuboid and check your answer.

Here are some ideas to get you started.

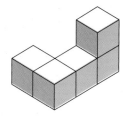 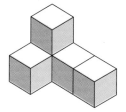 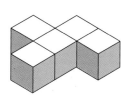 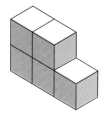

Repeat the activity several times, making a different shape each time.

B1 Work out the least number of cubes needed to make each shape into a cuboid.

a
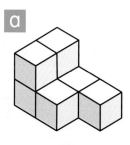

b
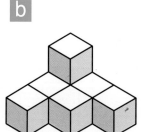

c
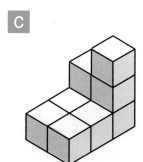

d
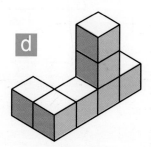

e
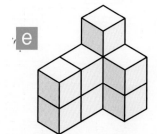

f
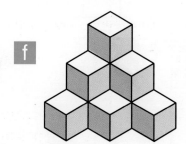

Symmetrical patterns

Key idea | You can reflect a pattern in more than 1 mirror line.

A1 You need CM 26 a mirror and red, black, yellow and blue pencils.

These unfinished patterns have 2 lines of symmetry at right angles.

Copy and complete each pattern.

Use a mirror to check your patterns.

Example

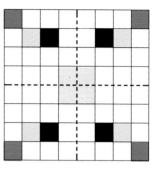

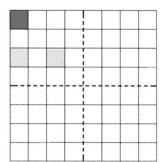

a

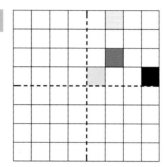

b

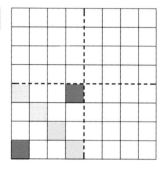

c

B1 You need CM 26, a mirror and red, black, yellow and blue pencils.

Copy the patterns and complete them so that each has the 2 lines of symmetry shown.

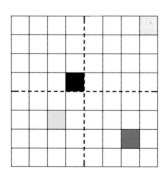

a

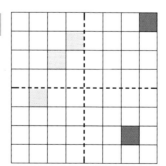

b

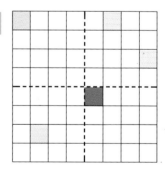

c

C1 This pattern uses half squares.

Copy and complete it.

C2 Make up your own patterns with 2 lines of symmetry. Use whole and half squares.

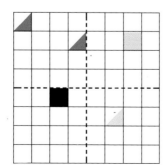

Take care with reflection of triangles.

SS 3.4 Symmetrical designs

Key idea	You can find reflective symmetry in the geometric designs of different cultures.

A1 | Tile designs

You need squared paper and red, black, yellow and blue pencils.

These unfinished tile designs have 2 lines of symmetry. Copy them on squared paper and complete them.

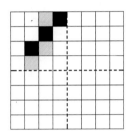

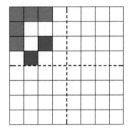

B1 | Tile designs and border patterns

You need squared paper.

a Draw an 8 by 8 grid.

Mark horizontal and vertical mirror lines.

Make your own design in one quarter of the grid.

Example

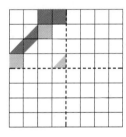

b Reflect your design in both mirror lines to make a tile.

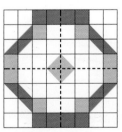

c Repeat the tile to make a border pattern.

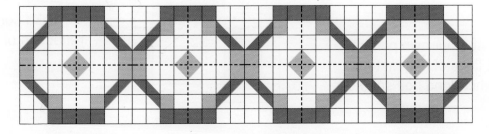

Larger tile designs

Draw all lines lightly in pencil so that you can rub some out later.

a Draw a 6 by 6 grid.

Draw horizontal and vertical mirror lines to split the grid into quarters.

Draw some lines to make a design in one of the quarters.

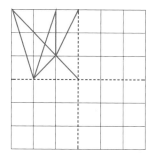

b Reflect your design in both mirror lines.

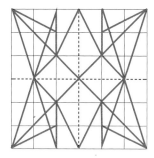

c Rub out lines to make a design that you find pleasing.

Make sure that you rub out the same lines in each quarter.

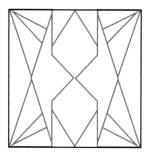

d Colour your design.

It should still have reflective symmetry.

e Repeat the design 4 times to make a larger tile.

Key idea You can find reflective symmetry in the geometric designs of different cultures.

Reasoning about reflective symmetry

Key idea	Some polyominoes and combinations of polyominoes have reflective symmetry.

 1   You need interlocking square tiles and squared paper.

You could use a mirror to test for symmetry.

A tetromino is made from 4 squares joined by their sides.

Use your square tiles to make 4 different tetrominoes.

Record them on 1 cm squared paper. Draw any lines of symmetry.

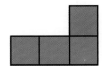

1   Shapes made from 5 squares are called pentominoes.

How many different pentominoes can you make?

There are 12 altogether.

Record as many as you can find on 1 cm squared paper.

Find pentominoes that have reflective symmetry and draw their lines of symmetry.

Example

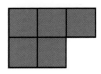

2   This symmetrical shape is made from 2 pentominoes.
There are 3 other ways of making the same shape using 2 pentominoes.

Make copies of your pentominoes on 2 cm squared paper and cut them out. See if you can find the other 3 ways.

Record them on 1 cm squared paper.

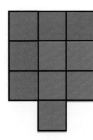

3   How many other symmetrical shapes made from 2 pentominoes can you find? Record them on 1 cm squared paper.

Draw the lines of symmetry.

C1   This rectangle is made from 3 different pentominoes.
How many other rectangles made from 3 different pentominoes can you find?

Record them on 1 cm squared paper.

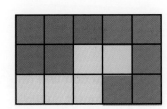

Border translations

Key idea	You can make repeating patterns by translating a shape a number of units to the left or the right

A1 You need squared paper.

In these border patterns, a red shape is translated.

Copy and continue each pattern.

How many units to the left or right is each shape translated.

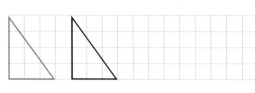

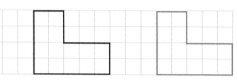

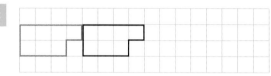

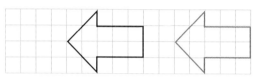

A2 Make your own border pattern by translating a shape.

B1 You need squared paper.

Make border patterns by translating each shape as follows:

a 2 units right
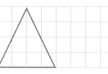

b 3 units left
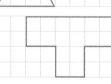

c 6 units right
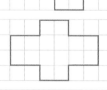

d 4 units left
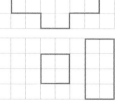

Colour your patterns.

C1 When will shapes in a border pattern

a overlap?   b just touch?   c have a gap between them?

Draw an example of each and write a rule.

SS 4.2 Translating polygons

Key idea	In a translation, every point moves the same number of units and in the same direction.

★1 You need CM 27.

Plot each point and then translate it. Mark the new point in a different colour and write its co-ordinates next to it.

	Starting point	Translation
a	(2, 3)	3 units right
b	(7, 6)	4 units left
c	(8, 1)	2 units up
d	(11, 8)	5 units down

A1 You need a blank copy of CM 27.

Plot the points and draw each shape on your grid.

Follow the instructions to translate the shape.

Describe the translation.

Example

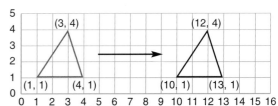

Add 9 to the x co-ordinates.
The shape has moved 9 units right.

a Add 6 to the x co-ordinates of shape A.

b Subtract 5 from the x co-ordinates of shape B.

c Add 6 to the y co-ordinates of shape C.

d Subtract 5 from the y co-ordinates of shape D.

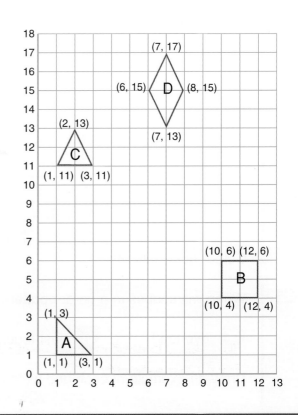

B1 You need a blank copy of CM 27.

- Draw this triangle on your grid.
  Label it A.

- Look at the instructions below and
  predict how the triangle will
  move each time.

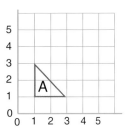

- Draw each new triangle and write the co-ordinates of its vertices.

  a Add 7 to the *x* co-ordinate of each vertex of triangle A to make triangle B.

  b Add 5 to the *y* co-ordinate of each vertex of triangle B to make triangle C.

  c Subtract 7 from the *x* co-ordinate of each vertex of triangle C to make triangle D.

  d Write an instruction to translate triangle D onto triangle A.

C1 You need a blank copy of CM 27.

Draw the square with co-ordinates
(1, 1), (4, 1), (4, 4) and (1, 4).

Investigate what happens when you

  a add the same number to **both** co-ordinates of each vertex,

  b subtract the same number from **both** co-ordinates of each vertex.

Write about what you find out.

Key idea | In a translation, every point moves the same number of units and in the same direction

SS 5.2 Diagonals

Key idea	A diagonal of a polygon is a straight line joining 2 non-adjacent vertices.

A1 You need shape templates.

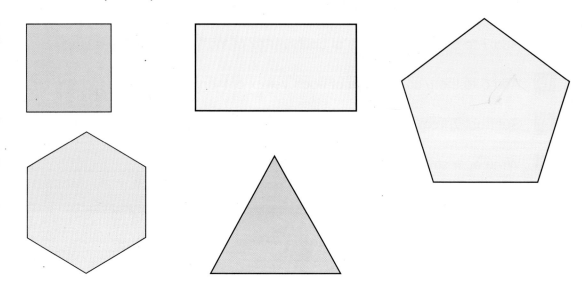

Draw these shapes.

How many diagonals can you draw from each vertex in each of the polygons?

How many diagonals are there altogether?

Make a table to show the name, number of sides, number of diagonals from each vertex and total number of diagonals of these polygons.

B1 Use shape templates.

How many diagonals can you draw from each vertex in these regular polygons?

How many diagonals are there altogether?

Record the name of the shape, the number of sides, the number of diagonals from each vertex and the total number of diagonals in a table.

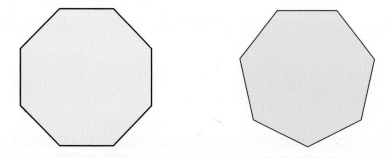

B2 What do you notice about the number of diagonals that can be drawn from a vertex of a polygon?

Making polygons rigid

Key idea | To make a polygon rigid, join vertices with diagonals that divide the shape into triangles.

A1 You need geostrips. Work in a group of 3 or 4.

  a Make triangles, rectangles and pentagons. Predict how many diagonals are needed to make each polygon rigid.

  b Now try it. How many diagonals do you need? Were your predictions correct? Keep a record by drawing the shapes and diagonals.

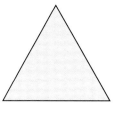  

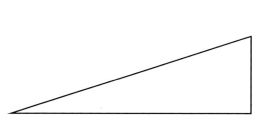 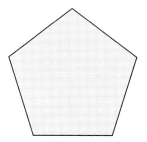

B1 You need geostrips. Work in a group of 3 or 4.

Make triangles, rectangles, pentagons, hexagons, heptagons and octagons. Find the smallest number of diagonals needed to make each polygon rigid.

Record your results in a table.

Keep your models to show the rest of the class.

C1 **a** Can you predict how many diagonals are needed to make a nonagon (9-sided polygon) rigid?

  b Try it!

C2 Make a general statement about the number of diagonals needed to make any polygon rigid.

SS 5.4 Plotting points on a grid

Key idea	To find a point in the first quadrant, use the *x*-axis and then the *y*-axis.

A1 You need squared paper.

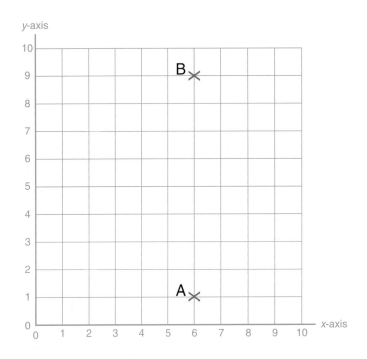

Copy the grid and label points A and B with their co-ordinates.

Join them to draw the vertical line AB.

A2 Plot points and join them to draw a line CD which is parallel to AB.

Label points C and D with their co-ordinates.

A3 Plot points F (1, 3) and G (9, 3), and join them to draw line FG.

Give co-ordinates of 2 more points on this line.

A4 Give the co-ordinates of the point where AB and FG cross.

A5 Plot points and join them to draw a diagonal line HI on the grid.
Label points H and I with their co-ordinates.

B1 You need squared paper.

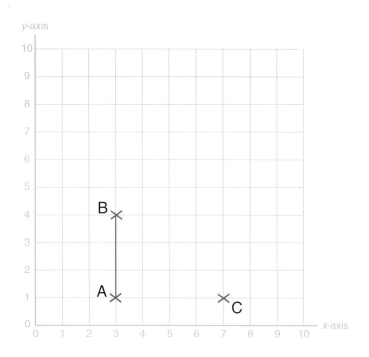

Copy this grid. Make line AB longer and give the co-ordinates of another point on it.

B2 Plot points to complete a line CD, which is parallel to AB.

B3 Plot points and draw a line EF. It is horizontal and starts at E (2, 2).

B4 Plot points and draw a line GH. It starts at G (2, 8) and is parallel to EF.

B5 Give the co-ordinates for the point where GH crosses CD. (You may need to extend CD.)

B6 Plot and draw the line IJ, where I is (1, 1), J is (6, 6). What type of line is this?

Give the co-ordinates of another point on this line.

C1 Write the co-ordinates of 4 points that lie on the line AB.
What do you notice about them?

C2 What can you say about the co-ordinates of any point on the line GH?

C3 If they were extended, would the lines AB and GH cross?

C4 Imagine the line IJ is extended on a larger grid. Give the co-ordinates of 4 more points that would be on the line. Explain how you know.

SS 5.5 Plotting vertices

| Key idea | By joining points in order, you can draw a 2-D shape on a grid. |

★1   You need squared paper.

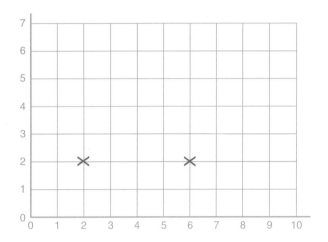

a   Copy the grid. Finish plotting these points and join them in order to make a 2-D shape:
(2, 2), (6, 2), (6, 6), (2, 6).

b   Name the shape.

A1   **Hidden shapes**

You need squared paper.

Draw a separate grid for each set of points. Plot the points and join them in order. Name the 2-D shapes.

a   (2, 2), (8, 2), (8, 6), (2, 6)

b   (2, 2), (6, 2), (2, 6)

c   (3, 2), (4, 6), (8, 6), (9, 2)

A2   Make a 'Hidden shape' puzzle for a friend.

B1   You need squared paper.

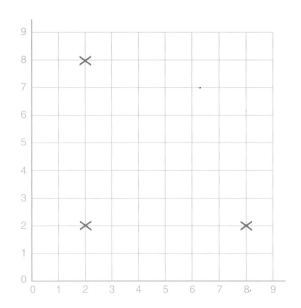

These co-ordinates are the vertices of a square.

One pair of co-ordinates is missing.

Find the position of the missing point and give its co-ordinates.

(2, 8) (2, 2) (8, 2) (☐ , ☐)

B2   Now try these. Draw each square on a separate grid.

a   (4, 2) (7, 2) (7, 5) (☐ , ☐)

b   (3, 5) (7, 5) (7, 9) (☐ , ☐)

B3   A (5, 4) and B (5, 7) are joined to make a straight line. It is one side of a square. Where could the other vertices be?

Show your answer on a grid.

Key idea   By joining points in order, you can draw a 2-D shape on a grid.

SS6.1 Identifying angles

C1

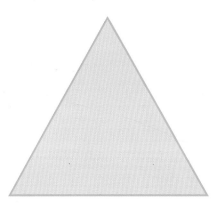

a Are the angles in this triangle acute or obtuse?

b Draw an example of a triangle with an obtuse angle.

c Try to draw a triangle with 2 obtuse angles.

What happens?

C2 a Draw a quadrilateral with 2 obtuse angles.

b Identify the other 2 angles.

c Is it possible to draw a quadrilateral with 3 obtuse angles? Try it and see.

C3 a Draw any pentagon and identify its angles.

b Can you draw a pentagon with more than 1 acute angle?

Measuring angles

| Key idea | You can use a protractor to measure an angle. |

B1 The robot needs to know the size of the marked angles in order to reach the treasure. Measure each angle to the nearest 5°.

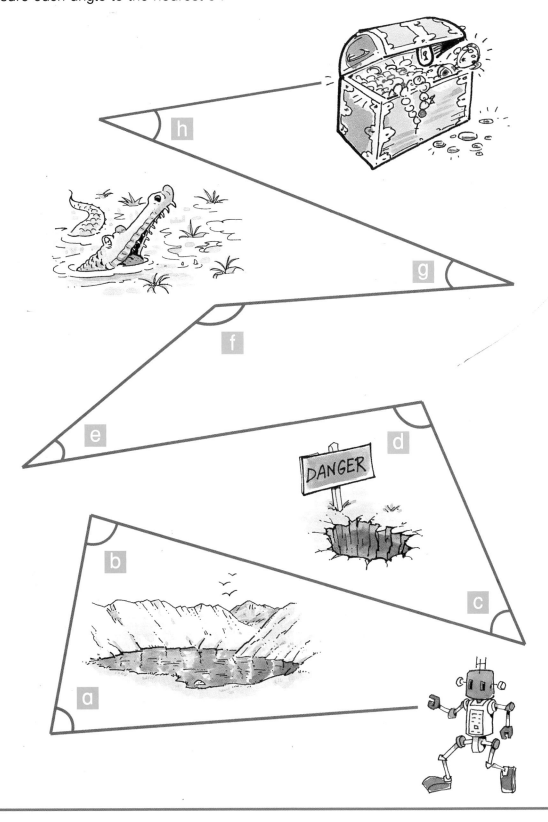

HD1.1 Chance

	Key idea	Probability is a way of describing the chance there is of something happening.

A1 Work with a partner.

Copy this table.

Look at the statements below.

Use the letter by each statement to record it in the right place in the table.

Impossible	Poor chance	Good chance	Certain

a It will rain this week.

b You are a year older now than you were this time last year.

c Your friend will play with you at breaktime.

d You will touch the ground at least once today.

e It will snow tomorrow.

f There will be 2 Decembers this year.

g You will leave this classroom before 6 p.m.

h You will see the sun shining through your window at midnight.

B1 You need cards from CM 40 and a partner.

Shuffle the cards.

Take turns to pick one from the pile and make a statement that fits the card.

If your partner agrees, write the chance word or phrase and your statement in your book.

C1

Play 'Misfits':

You need cards from CM 41 and a partner.

Shuffle the cards and divide them into 2 equal piles with the pictures face down.

Take turns to pick up a card from each pile and join them together. Repeat until all the cards have been used.

Score 2 points if you make a whole, matching picture and 1 point if you have a top and a bottom card, but they don't match.

The winner is the player with the most points when all the cards have been used.

C2

What chance have you of making

 a   a whole, matching picture?

 b   a whole picture that doesn't match?

C3

How could you improve your chances of picking up a whole picture?

Write down your ideas.

Key idea	Likelihood means 'how likely' something is to happen.

★1 Use the picture on page 78 to help you with A.

A1 You need a partner.

Discuss and record something that:

a is certain to happen   b may happen

c is possible   d is impossible

e is likely to happen   f is unlikely to happen

B1 You need a partner, CM 42 and scissors.

Cut out cards from CM 42.

Play 'Likelihood' with your partner:

• Mix up the cards and lay them out face down.

• Take turns to pick up a card. Use the words on the card to begin a sentence for your partner to finish.

C1 Make up sentences that include these words:

very likely   probable   possible   **unlikely**

more likely   uncertain   **highly probable**

HD2.1 What is the problem?

Key idea	A hypothesis says what you think is happening.

A1 Arthur thinks that most of the children in his class get to school in less than 10 minutes.

His hypothesis is: Most children in my class take less than 10 minutes to get to school.

He collects some information and makes this tally chart:

Tally chart to show the time children take to get to school

less than 10 minutes	ⳘⳘⳘ
10 minutes or more	ⳘⳘ

a   How many children take less than 10 minutes to get to school?

b   How many children take 10 minutes or more to get to school?

c   Is Arthur right? Do most of the children get to school in under 10 minutes?

A2 Andrea thinks that most of the children in her class take 10 minutes or more to get to school.

a   What is Andrea's hypothesis?

b   Here is a bar chart of the data she collects.

Do most children take 10 minutes or more to get to school? Is Andrea's hypothesis correct?

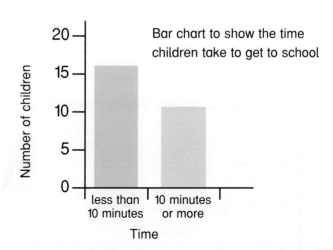

Bar chart to show the time children take to get to school

B1 Pat's school is thinking of making lunchtime shorter.

Pat thinks that most of the children in her class would not mind if 15 minutes was cut from lunchtime.

She writes this hypothesis:

Most children in my class would not mind if the lunchtime was 15 minutes shorter.

She asked children to say how much time they would cut from lunchtime.

Here is the information she collected from her class:

Tally chart to show how much time children would cut from lunchtime.

0 minutes	5 minutes	10 minutes	15 minutes
~~HHH~~ IIII	~~HHH~~ I	~~HHH~~ II	~~HHH~~ ~~HHH~~

a How many children would not mind if 15 minutes was cut from lunchtime?

b How many children altogether wanted less than 15 minutes to be cut from lunchtime?

Count up all the children who chose less than 15 minutes.

c Which did more children want, a cut of 15 minutes or a cut of less than 15 minutes?

d Was Pat's hypothesis correct?

B2 a Do you think most children in your class would mind if 15 minutes was cut from lunchtime and they could go home 15 minutes earlier? Write your own hypothesis.

b Draw a tally chart like this to find out.
Ask 10 children what they think.

Would mind if lunchtime was 15 minutes shorter	Would NOT mind if lunchtime was 15 minutes shorter

c Was your hypothesis correct?

C1 Think of your own hypothesis. It can be about anything you like, as long as

* it makes a prediction: *I think that ...*
* you would be able to test it by gathering information from children in your class.

For example, it could be about how children travel to school, 'I think most children walk', about their hobbies, 'I think that more children play football than chess' or about the type of pet they may have.

C2 Write down your hypothesis and say what information you would need to collect to test it.

HD 3.2 Finding the mode and the range

> **Key idea** | In a set of data, the range is the difference between the maximum and minimum values.

★1 Which is the most popular colour?

The mode is_____.

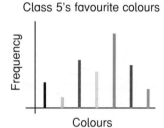

Class 5's favourite colours

Frequency

Colours

★2 Find the most common number of brothers and sisters.

Tally chart of children in Year 5.
How many brothers and sisters?

0	卌 卌 卌 卌
1	卌 卌 卌 卌 卌 卌 IIII
2	卌 卌 卌 卌 III
3	卌 IIII
4	II
5	I

The mode is_____.

A1 These are the shoe sizes of a group of children in Class 5.

  a What is the mode of the shoe sizes?

  b What is the range of the shoe sizes?

A2 Find the mode and the range of each set of data.

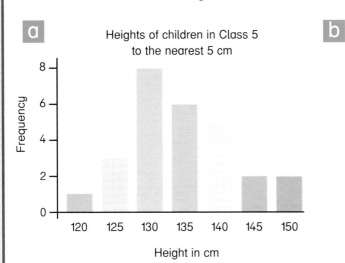

a

Heights of children in Class 5
to the nearest 5 cm

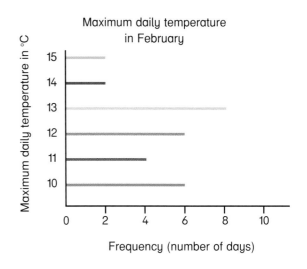

b

Maximum daily temperature
in February

B1 You need a partner, one poetry book and one reference book between you, and squared paper.

Test this hypothesis

> We think that longer words are used more often in reference books than in poetry books.

a Collect your data quickly.

- Have one book each.

- Choose a typical page.

- Count the number of letters in each of its first 50 words, keeping a tally as you do so.

Typical means
'one that is like a lot of
the rest'.

b Draw a bar chart or a bar line chart on squared paper.

c Find the mode and the range of your data.

d Compare your findings with your partner's.

e Do you think the hypothesis is correct?

Give as many reasons as you can.

You need squared paper.

a Draw a bar line chart showing data with a mode of 5 and a range of 4.

b Draw a bar line chart showing data with a mode of 5 and a range of 9.

Don't forget to label the axes and give your chart a title. The picture may help with ideas.

Key idea	In a set of data, the range is the difference between the maximum and minimum values.

D 3.3 Using a database 2

Key idea | A database is a collection of information stored in an organised way, for example in a table or on a computer.

1 Work in a group. You each need CM 51.

Fill in your information on the top line of the database sheet.

When you have completed it, pass your sheet to the person to your left.

Your sheet should get back to you once everyone in your group has filled it in.

- a Which type of book is most popular in your group?
- b Which author is most popular?
- c Which authors do you think the library should definitely have?
- d Was any subject for non-fiction books chosen by more than one person?
- e Is any subject for non-fiction books especially popular?

2 Swap half of your group's database sheets with half of those from another group, so that you have some of your sheets and some of theirs. Share one of their sheets with a partner.

- a Use the other group's sheet to answer question 1 a – e
- b Were their choices similar to the ones made by your group?

3 Look at the data from both groups.

- a Are there any authors that you think the library should definitely have?
- b Which subjects for non-fiction books are popular?

4 You need squared paper.

a Use all the information from both groups' database sheets to draw a bar line chart that shows the types of book chosen.

b Use your chart to make recommendations for the library.

C1 If there was only one suggestion that could be carried out by the library, which do you think it should be? Why?

C2 Write to the library suggesting the books you think they should have for children of your age. Use any of the information you have found out to give reasons for your choices.

Key idea	A database is a collection of information stored in an organised way, for example in a table or on a computer.

D 3.4 Interpreting line graphs

Key idea | A line graph shows patterns clearly but not exactly what happens between each point.

This graph shows the sales of children's books at Brown's Bookshop:

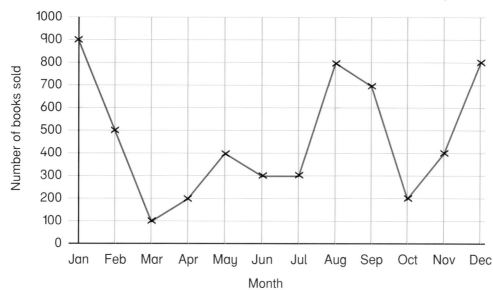

★1 How many books were sold in January?

★2 How many books were sold in March?

★3 In which months did they sell ⓐ 500 books? ⓑ 700 books? ⓒ 300 books?

A1 ⓐ When were sales of children's books high?

ⓑ Why do you think this happened?

A2 When were sales at their lowest? Can you think of a reason why?

A3 ⓐ How many children's books were sold in July?

ⓑ How many children's books were sold in August?

ⓒ How many more books were sold in August than July?

A4 Which month had the same number of sales as May?

This graph shows the sales of children's books at Brown's Bookshop:

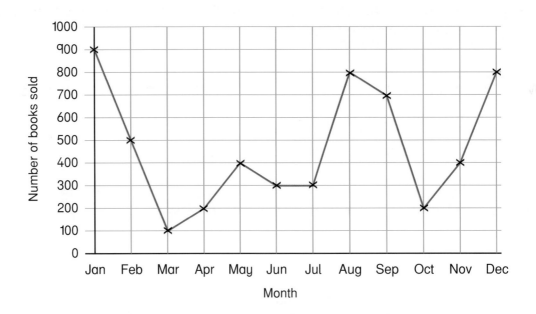

This graph shows the sales of adults' books at Brown's Bookshop:

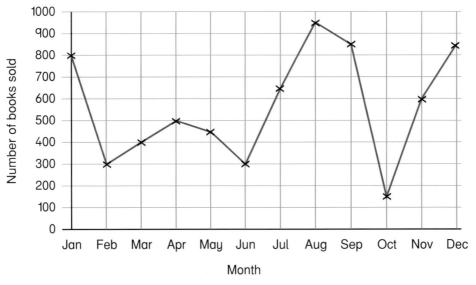

B1 Compare these 2 graphs.

     a   In what ways are the 2 graphs similar?

     b   In what ways are they different?

B2 Sales for May were plotted halfway between 400 and 500 books. What were the sales for May?

B3 Which month had sales of 650 books?

B4 Between which months did sales fall the most?

C1 You need CM 52.

Using the information from both graphs on page 88, draw a new graph which shows the total sales of children's and adults' books.

C2 Which month showed the greatest number of sales? How many books were sold?

C3 When did sales increase most rapidly?

C4 If you owned this shop, when might you take your holiday? Why?

Key idea A line graph shows patterns clearly but not exactly what happens between each point.

Testing a hypothesis

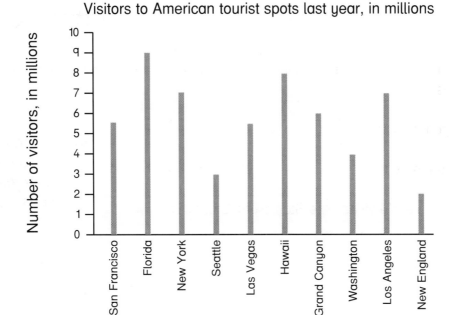

Visitors to American tourist spots last year, in millions

A1 This bar line chart shows visitor numbers at 10 tourist spots in the USA.

a Which was the most popular place to visit?

b Which was the least popular of the ten?

c Which 2 places were equally popular?

A2 Approximately how many people visited a Seattle? b New York? c Florida?

A3 Which of these 3 places, New York, Florida or Las Vegas, do you think would be most popular to visit for the 8 people sitting nearest to you? Make a hypothesis and test it. Were you right?

B1 Look at the bar line chart above.

a Approximately how many people visited the Grand Canyon?

b Approximately how many more people visited Florida than Las Vegas?

c Approximately how many people altogether visited these 10 tourist spots?

B2 This table gives data for visitors to the Statue of Liberty in New York last year.

Month	Jan	Feb	Mar	Apr	May	Jun	Jul	Aug	Sep	Oct	Nov	Dec
Number of visitors (hundred thousands)	2	2	5	3.5	6	11	11	6	4	4	3.2	2.4

You need squared paper.

a Make a bar line chart to show this information and use it to answer the remaining questions.

b Which months had the greatest number of visitors?

c Which had the least? Can you think of a reason why?

d How many people visited the Statue of Liberty last year?

> Remember, the chart shows numbers in hundreds of thousands!

B3 Why do you think most people visit the Statue of Liberty in June and July? Write a hypothesis. What information would you need to test your hypothesis?

C1 Compare the number of visitors to New York with the number of visitors to the Statue of Liberty.

Why do you think fewer people visited the Statue of Liberty than visited New York?

> The Statue of Liberty is in New York.

C2 What data could be represented in this bar chart?

Choose a suitable topic and

a create a tally chart,

b decide on a scale and copy the chart,

c label the axes and give it a title.

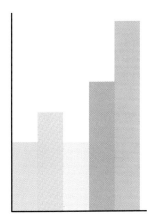

Key idea | Organised data is easier to understand.

HD 4.2   Using the mode and the range

Key idea	You can use the mode and the range to compare sets of data.

A1   Look at the chart.

Hours of sunshine each day for a week

Resort 1	4	6	8	8	2	5	7
Resort 2	6	7	9	9	7	9	4
Resort 3	5	3	3	4	3	7	5

What is the mode for

a   resort 1?   b   resort 2?   c   resort 3?

> The mode is the most common number or item.

A2   What is the maximum number of hours of sunshine for

a   resort 1?   b   resort 2?   c   resort 3?

A3   What is the minimum number of hours of sunshine for

a   resort 1?   b   resort 2?   c   resort 3?

A4   What is the range of temperature for

a   resort 1?   b   resort 2?   c   resort 3?

> The range is the difference between the maximum and minimum values.

B1   Sometimes it rains!

Rainfall in centimetres each day for a week

Resort 1	1	0	0	0	2	2	1
Resort 2	2	1	0	0	0	0	2
Resort 3	0	4	3	5	3	0	0

What is the mode of rainfall for

a   resort 1?   b   resort 2?   c   resort 3?

B2   What is the range of rainfall for

a   resort 1?   b   resort 2?   c   resort 3?

B3 You need to look at the information on IP23, as well as at the charts below.

Hours of sunshine each day for a week

Resort 1	4	6	8	8	2	5	7
Resort 2	6	7	9	9	7	9	4
Resort 3	5	3	3	4	3	7	5

Rainfall in centimetres each day for a week

Resort 1	1	0	0	0	2	2	1
Resort 2	2	1	0	0	0	0	2
Resort 3	0	4	3	5	3	0	0

a Make a table of the mode and range for temperature, hours of sunshine and rainfall for the 3 resorts.

	Resort 1		Resort 2		Resort 3	
	M	R	M	R	M	R
T (°C)						
S (h)						
R(cm)						

b Which resort would you choose for a beach holiday?

c Why? Give 3 reasons, using the mode and range to compare the weather in the resorts.

C1

a Think about other sorts of data to compare by finding the mode and the range.

b Discuss your ideas with a partner.

Write down the best ones.

Key idea You can use the mode and the range to compare sets of data.

HD 4.3 Using a database 3

B1 Read this information taken from a brochure.

Southwich has a sandy beach, and the mode temperature is 18 °C in summer. There is a children's play area as well as a park with a boating lake. There is a museum and a castle.

Westwick has a pebble beach and a mode temperature of 20 °C in summer. There is a fairground and children's play area. There is a castle.

Eastwell has no beach, and a mode temperature of 20 °C in summer. There is a children's play area, a fairground and a park. There is a museum.

Northway has a sandy beach and a mode temperature of 14 °C in summer. There is a park with a boating lake. There is a castle.

a Which resort would you like to stay at?

b Why?

B2 You need CM 55.

a Make a database for the information in B1.

b Look at it carefully.

Think about your answer to B1 **a** again.

Change your mind if you want to.

c Answer B1 **b** again, but this time use more detail from the database.

B3 Which resort has the best facilities for

a young children (under 7)? **b** teenagers? **c** adults without children?

C1 You need some travel brochures and CM 55.

Choose 3 hotels and make your own database.

C2 Use your database to answer the questions in B3.

ID 4.4 Comparing line graphs

Key idea	Line graphs are a good way of representing and comparing 2 sets of similar data.

Holiday destination	Temperature in °C											
	Jan	Feb	Mar	Apr	May	Jun	Jul	Aug	Sep	Oct	Nov	Dec
Barcelona, Spain	13	14	16	18	21	25	28	28	25	21	17	13
Madrid, Spain	9	11	15	19	22	27	31	32	25	18	13	9
Seville, Spain	15	18	21	24	27	32	36	38	32	26	20	16
Palma de Mallorca	14	15	17	19	22	26	29	29	27	23	18	15
Gran Canaria	22	22	22	23	27	25	24	25	26	25	23	21
Orlando, Florida	20	22	26	28	33	31	33	33	33	29	25	22
Miami, Florida	24	24	27	29	32	31	33	33	32	30	27	24

★1 You need CM 56.

Draw a line graph of temperature in Madrid.

★2 Use your graph and the graph of temperature in Barcelona on IP 24 to decide when it is

hottest in   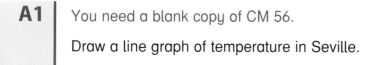 Barcelona,   b Madrid.

★3 Which of the 2 places has the

a warmer winters?   b   warmer summers?

c most months over 20 °C?

A1 You need a blank copy of CM 56.

Draw a line graph of temperature in Seville.

A2 Compare this with the graph of temperature in Barcelona on IP24.

a Which has the hotter May?

b Which has more months with a temperature over 20 °C?

c Which would be better for a holiday during the winter months?

B1 You need 2 blank copies of CM 56.

    a Draw a line graph of temperature in Orlando, Florida.

    b Draw a line graph of temperature in Miami, Florida.

B2 Make 5 statements comparing the data in the graphs for Miami and Orlando.

C1 Add the Miami data to the graph for Orlando.

> Use a different colour when you draw a second line graph on the same pair of axes.

C2 Which do you think is better, comparing graphs on the same or on different axes?

Make a list of the good and bad points of each method.